KV-433-443

Patricia Collins is a writer, editor, designer and illustrator. Born in 1936 at Governor's Island, New York, she received a BA in Philosophy and Art from the College of New Rochelle and a master's degree in Fine Art and Education from Pratt Institute in New York. From 1966, together with her husband Tom, she has been involved in all aspects of editorial development for books published under the Collins' own imprint.

MARY
A Mother's Story

PATRICIA COLLINS

SPHERE BOOKS LIMITED
30-32 Gray's Inn Road, London WC1X 8JL

First published in Great Britain by
Sphere Books Ltd 1981
Copyright © Patricia Collins 1980

TRADE
MARK

Printed and bound in Great Britain by
©ollins, Glasgow

[It was] a little thing, the size of a hazelnut, which seemed to lie in the palm of my hand; and it was as round as any ball. I looked upon it with the eye of my understanding, and thought, 'What may this be?' I was answered in a general way, thus: 'It is all that is made.' I wondered how long it could last: for it seemed as though it might suddenly fade away to nothing, it was so small.

Foreword

There is something unique about the suffering of each parent who has a handicapped child. And yet there is a similarity – a pattern – in that terrible period of time between the initial refusal to face the child's disability and the later acceptance. I tried to hide all my real thoughts and feelings during that interval. I think most parents do, in their different ways.

I expect that people who read this and have a disabled child will take some comfort in seeing that there is nothing unusual in their anger, bitterness, and resentment – strong and mean feelings mixed up in their hearts with nobler emotions. I hope that parents ashamed of their reactions in similar circumstances will take courage from the fact that a woman who railed as hard as I did – who was so totally unwilling to accept the fact of a little girl's brain damage and its consequences – nevertheless found new vision, new hope, new life precisely through that little child.

It wasn't easy to recall exactly the way I felt those days and months and years. I had so covered it up that going back over it was like lifting a heavy stone. Underneath the stone I discovered all sorts of dark things – live things buried there, things that scurried from the sunlight. I think most parents will understand how much I wanted to put the stone back. Instead I lifted it once and for all. I wrote it all down.

What Tom, my husband, did – he took the pile of raw pages, full of half-articulated experiences and accounts of shameful emotions, and with his pencil laboriously went over the sheets, editing and rewriting and rearranging the bits and pieces. The two of us went back and forth over it, trying to make a richer and more readable account of this strangest episode in our lives. We agree that the book is wholly my work and also all his.

Janet and John Marqusee have our gratitude for giving their enthusiasm and great support to the project, David Lubell for knowing they would, Margaret Mohns for selflessly dedicating herself to the work of preparing the manuscript and Liz Wilhide for doing such superb work as editor.

The point of it all is that a journey was made through wild spaces of the mind yet a quiet shore was reached, and what looked like a curse came to seem a blessing. If I had my choice now – if a white light came into the room, and from the light a voice came saying that all of what passed was to be erased, that Mary were to be whole and healthy without any brain damage whatever – my joy would be beyond describing. But I would ask, for myself, one thing more. I would ask not to have to go back to my old ways of thinking and feeling. I would never want to unlearn what I have learned from Mary.

Patricia Collins

Homecoming

My watch said one-thirty. I stared at it in the dim light and blinked. Only an hour and a half past midnight, New York time, yet the plane was moving into the dawn. I slid open the plastic window shutter and peered out at the brightening sky. Below were white cobblestones of cloud. The horizon was a line of red gold, heralding the sun. When the plane, after a stop at Shannon, would cross Ireland and land at the airport north of Dublin, it would be nine-thirty in the morning, Irish time. Though I had slept only two hours or so, I would have to find energy to deal with a whole new day.

I set my watch forward five hours and wondered whether to shutter the window and try to sleep again. But the stewardesses were busy in the galley. I could hear them opening and closing the metal doors with soft thuds as they gathered together the rudiments of a light breakfast.

I clasped my hands in my lap. My fingers were still sticky with rubber cement, from my work in New York, where I'd been pasting down the last of the illustrations for a photobook. I could feel the stuff around my nails. There were India ink stains on the callus of the middle finger of my right hand. All that day in the office in New York I'd been inking crop marks on the big white sheets covered with type and photostats. I'd worked until the last moment so that the paste-ups would be ready for the printer.

I picked at my fingers, peeling off more of the tiny gummy strips, rolling the new yield of rubber cement into a little ball. The month in New York had taught me that things were not going well.

I

A stewardess was moving down the aisle now as the passengers lowered their shelves and clicked them into place. I decided to forget sleep, to accept a tray and settle back to pick at the threads and pieces of my worrying. I took a second stewardess's bright good morning and the black coffee that came with it. I set down my hot cup and fiddled with a paper-covered bun, looking for a clue to its unwrapping.

At Kennedy, Tom had seemed confident. *Was* confident, of course; that was his way. We'd been married now for nearly ten years and had worked together for eight of those years in our own company – The Business, we called it. I poured cream in my coffee and stirred it, looking vaguely into the whorls. I pictured Tom in New York, pacing the office, smoking too many cigarettes. 'Not to worry,' he would keep saying. He liked this phrase Irish people used so much. Tom found the Irish charming. But it did not encourage me to be reminded of their lightly given promises and their loose anchorless hoping.

I sipped the coffee, put the cup down, pushed the shutter back and stared out at the cold clouds. *Mañana* people is what they were, whistlers in the dark. Of course it would not be the fault of the Irish if all our meetings and arrangements in America and Europe led to nothing. I felt a shudder, like a small wave of ice in my stomach, as I thought of the truly awful failure of the audiovisual project I'd come to Ireland to work on ten months ago. It was to have been the sustaining project for our modest Dublin establishment, paying setup and staff costs, paying the rent for the big enough house, on the seafront in Sandycove, with its unobstructed view of the Martello tower of James Joyce's *Ulysses*.

This audiovisual project involved a package of twelve educational filmstrips with accompanying teacher book-

2

lets. Now of course I could have done the work in New York, could have done it anywhere. But Tom had excogitated a romantic notion that Ireland would provide us with both a home and a base for an overseas publishing adventure he had in mind, using European sources to generate books to sell in the American and world markets. What more natural mid-Atlantic locale than Ireland, straddling the air highway between North America and Europe?

One night in February last year I sat up with him till three in the morning trying to talk him out of this notion. I was two months pregnant then. It's not a good idea, I argued, to move now. Let's wait a year.

It was a time, though, when New York women were very aggressive about pregnancy. They'd play tennis in maternity sports togs and jog along, humpty dumpty of figure but light of mind, to classes where natural childbirth was taught. I recall seeing in my alumnae quarterly a picture of an administrative assistant whose glory was that she breastfed her newborn infant at the college, on the job. So I couldn't let a little thing like pregnancy throw Tom's plan off, could I? And Tom, like our daughter Bonnie after him, had an effective way of being stubborn about what he wanted to do. When either of them would get caught up in some enterprise, they'd just set their faces in a wide smile and plunge right ahead. Yet to tell the truth I was drawn, myself, by the lure of Tom's idea of Ireland. It was the home of my forebears as well as his, a place of magical associations in old family stories and apocrypha. I imagined a certain simplicity. We'd have a calm refuge far from frenetic New York. I'd have a respite from the responsibility of the expensive oversized house on the north New Jersey coast where we then lived. And, for the audiovisual project, I'd be able to hire artists to help with all the work – and wages would be lower in Ireland. Surely,

3

too, I'd find all the happy-minded young Irish girls I'd need to help look after the children.

So I played along with Tom's scheme. We moved to Ireland in May; I gathered a staff and began work. All went well at first. Tom and I had approvals from the American producer for our first six scripts. But in July I began to hear nervous noises from the producer's editor, a blonde redfaced women with cold blue eyes. She seemed to dislike the second six scripts. Then more trouble: She asked for basic revisions of the six scripts she'd accepted earlier, for which I'd already done finished art frames. She was worried, too, about some of the visual interpretations of abstract concepts. I made wild efforts to rework scripts and art to suit her ever-changing instructions. 'She doesn't know what she wants,' one of our editors said: 'and she doesn't know what she *doesn't* want until she sees it.' In trying to satisfy her, I did enough work between May and November to complete the project three times over. Finally, in November, Tom and I decided to cut our losses, write the whole thing off, declare it a dead letter. The balance due and owing for the work (virtually all finished) would now never be paid. Meanwhile, Tom's European ventures, with all *their* promise, were yielding very little. We, or rather I, began to feel terribly exposed: the heavy borrowings from banks; the publishers who weren't gambling, the various people who were draining our resources. Tom blamed the Nixon economy and Arthur Burns. I blamed the Arabs, the effects of whose oil embargo became vivid to me during the chill Irish winter. A time of black luck for us. But Tom and I both knew that in large part we were responsible.

Sitting in the plane, finishing my coffee, I felt suddenly and inappropriately comforted by the warmth flooding in and around me. The sun was burning on the horizon now, a

4

rich yellow as it rose higher. Shafts of light suffused the cabin, dissolving remorse and fear. I could see the three children, Bonnie and Mark and Mary, vivid and marvellous in my mind's eye. Bonnie, who was nearly eight years old, blue-eyed and smiling, holding little Mary, now eight months old; Mark, five, tickling Mary's toes or pulling at Bonnie's long brown hair, making mischief while Nannie gently scolded . . .

The trolley moved back up the aisle and the girls collected the trays. The senior hostess, her jacket on, in a quick impulsive movement seized the microphone.

'Welcome to Ireland,' she said, in a warm authoritative voice.

An hour and a half later, after the plane had arced from Shannon to Dublin, I'd collected my things and passed through Customs and Immigration and was settled in a rattling black taxi heading towards Dublin. After another forty minutes' drive through city traffic and on out the smooth winding southern road, I searched along the line of seacoast suburban homes and saw, around a curve, the tall bluish grey house in Sandycove. The winds carried great clouds in swift strides across the sky. The sky over the sea out here was always changing – sun and shade, rain and sun and rainbow often following in succession on a single morning. The tide had pushed high up against the seawall, the water lapping languidly against the stones. That lapping sound – how had I forgotten it? – made me happy. The wooden house, though a jerrybuilt semi-detached structure, stood boldly in its place at the corner, a few feet above the sea road.

I left the cab, paid the driver, hoisted my bags and pressed through the swinging wooden gate set in the waist-high stone wall. I made my way along the pebbled path to the booth-like protective enclosure. Pushing in with the bags, I lifted the knocker and let it fall against the door.

There was silence, then excited shrieks and the thumping of feet down the hallway.

The door swung open, and Bonnie and Mark stood there.

'Mommy! Mommy!' they shouted, bouncing up and down. There was a shower of chatter. I dropped my bags, hugged them both hard and stepped back for a long look. Bonnie had always been a socially precocious and independent child. I was struck by the Irishness of this new Bonnie. Not only were her speech patterns and her intonations Irish; she was already Irish even in the tilt of her head and her smile.

'What did you bring us?' Mark asked, as his eyes fell to the bags behind me.

'Presents. Little ones.'

'Oh!' he said, his brown eyes shining under the blond curls.

'First let me get a good look at you.'

Marlene, my assistant, had said during a transatlantic call a week earlier that Mark had been sick and the doctor had been to see him.

'How have you been, Mark?' I asked.

'I've been getting bigger,' he said proudly.

Bonnie was as gregarious as an orchestra. Mark, with his quick dark brown eyes, was a soloist. He was always brewing some hypothesis or wild plan, some construct of birth, death, God or the devil. He'd be off by himself making a pulley system to haul toys up the stairwell. He'd build complex block roadways or stretch strings in intricate webbings across a floor. He'd take all the spices and condiments in the kitchen and mix them up into what he called a Sergeant Pepper. On weekend mornings in recent months he'd taken to riding around the neighbourhood in the milkman's wagon, saying it was his 'job'.

There was a two-step elevation which formed a landing

6

below the bay window. I lifted the bags to the window seat and Bonnie began to unzip them. I sat down on the stairs, just as Marlene came forward down the lower hallway, that little ironic grin of hers playing about the corners of her mouth.

'Hi, Boss,' Marlene said.

She'd called me 'Boss' ever since my short stay in the hospital before little Mary's birth. She'd been helping manage things for me at home, and would visit me every day. She came in the first day, her grin wider than usual. 'What's so funny?' I asked. 'Oh, I met a friend at the bus stop. I told him I was going to visit my boss. He asked where my boss's office was. "In the maternity hospital!" I said.' After that she'd always come in, draw up a chair and say, 'Well, *Boss*, here's what went wrong today . . .'

An American in her mid-twenties, Marlene had been living in Europe for several years. She'd turned up a month or so after our arrival in Dublin and began working for us as a secretary. She helped not only with the studio and office work but also with the cooking and the kitchen and the shopping. Marlene also made granola and tended a little garden.

'How has everything been?' I was asking now.

'Well, pretty *good* on the whole. But I felt like quitting several times.'

'Don't tell me a thing more!' I said.

'Is this for us, Mommy?' Bonnie had seized a stapled paper bag and was holding it aloft.

'Yes.'

'Goody!' She and Mark went to work to rip the package open. They plunked down on the landing and began to tear at the wrappings of their presents.

'And Nannie – ?'

'She's in with Mary,' Marlene answered, finding a perch on the window seat next to the open bags.

'Mark looks good now,' I said.

'Yep. We fixed him up. All he needed was that cherry medicine again.'

'And Mary?'

'Just fine and dandy.'

Mark, standing on the stair way beside me, patted my hair.

'Fuzzy,' he said.

'Yes.' My hair, always very curly in the damp Irish weather, had already massed atop my head.

I walked down the hall and into little Mary's room. She was awake on Nannie's bed, on her back, a pacifier pinned to her yellow terry suit, the one with the ducks on it. At her head and sides Nannie had wedged her with pillows and blanket rolls. The room was very warm and smelled of powder and baby lotion. Nannie looked up from where she sat, her thin frame sagging. She set her coffee cup on the bedside table, nodded to me, then turned to Mary. She patted Mary's stomach and stroked her head. '*Look* who's *here*!' she said, her voice full of forced enthusiasm.

Our dear, faithful, generous old Nannie! She was 'over sixty-five' when she'd come to us eight years earlier. We used to try occasionally to find out exactly how old Nannie was. But she wouldn't say. She would just laugh and make a remark like, 'Oh, old enough.' Tom once suggested I look at her passport. But I never did, and she never told.

It was Tom who had discovered Nannie, when Bonnie was six months old and a dark young girl from the West Indies – the last in a long line of inadequate babysitters – had quit, to fly home 'to visit a sick aunt'. At the time there was a special urgency: We'd planned to go to Europe shortly on a three-week business trip.

'A real nanny,' Tom finally said. 'That's what we need. We've got to go to the sisterhood.' Soon after, on a nearby street corner in mid-Manhattan where we then lived, he spied two women standing talking. They wore starched nurses' uniforms, and each of them presided over a blue English baby carriage, 'as large,' Tom said, 'as an aircraft carrier.'

They listened to his story.

'I know someone,' one of them told Tom. 'She's planning to retire, I think. But maybe she'd consider your little Bonnie. She's very good. She's the one I always leave my babies with when I have to take time off. She spoils the little ones a bit, but I'd rather have that – '

When Tom returned that afternoon he announced to me, and to Bonnie, that he'd found someone perfect for her – 'a nanny's nanny' was the way he put it. He'd phoned her, and she arrived that very evening. She sat straight up on the couch, a thin, serious, soft-spoken old woman, keeping her coat on, and her dark hat, its brim down over her hair. She didn't do any housework or cooking, she said, almost apologetically. She only took care of baby. That was the way she'd always worked; she'd always been a professional baby nurse. After our conversation she met Bonnie. Her delight in the baby was evident immediately.

It was with few qualms that we flew off to Europe a week afterwards.

In the months following our return I learned only a little more about Nannie. She'd arrived in America as a young girl from the west of Ireland, and had gone to work as a nurse, caring chiefly for children of prominent New England families. In later years she'd settled in New York City; she kept a room in a women's residence there. She was an avid newspaper reader, determinedly *au courant* with the latest social and political gossip, and was a great devotee of the soothsayer Jeanne Dixon. She read *The New York Times* and all the tabloids, even *The National Enquirer*.

9

Her reading and radio listening kept her abreast of the latest theories on child care.

Yet it didn't take me very long to discover that beneath Nannie's quiet intelligence lurked a stubborn selflessness which drove her to unreasonable extremes. She would nightly handwash little things that could have been machine washed. Day and night she would indulge a baby, rocking or carrying it around whenever it awoke, or repeatedly feeding it warm milk, until finally the infant fell asleep. She had her special ways of preparing food to make it painless to eat – scraping meat, mashing fruit. She spared no effort to make their little lives comfortable.

Nannie stayed on with us through thick and thin, through the years. There were times we couldn't pay her very much, and not paying her much began to be the rule. 'When you can, you can give me the difference,' she'd say, her concern first for Bonnie and then for Mark overriding any monetary self-interest. She became one of the family, she became a friend, though she'd always insist on keeping a certain professional distance.

Now, more than seven years after she'd come to us, her care of little Mary had finally exhausted her.

If Marlene hadn't been there to keep an eye on things this time, I never could have left the children with Nannie. I had too many images of Nannie, with her hair wisping over her face, her dress mussed from having fallen asleep with the baby on her lap; Nannie, at two in the morning, staggering around sleepily, trying to get her bearings as she made her way to the refrigerator to get yet another bottle of formula and heat it.

I leaned over Mary, who gave me a delighted smile, her little arms moving as she wriggled with pleasure. I picked her up and held her and felt her small warm head against my cheek. She laughed while I nibbled on her ear, pretending to eat her up. Finally I put her back on the bed again, sat down and studied this miracle child, born nearly three months too soon.

Unborn, Mary had been unreal, remote. But when she was only seconds old I saw her little face for the first time, so tiny but with that fascination only the human face has. It was a dusty pink face with tight shut eyes, with a sweet tiny mouth and little furled lips. The doctor held her aloft, her whole little being was cupped in his two gloved hands, her infinitesimal chin resting in the arc between his thumb and forefinger. It was then that she became utterly precious to me. I knew then how a primitive could worship a face he'd carved in stone or wood; and why a sketched circle enclosing three dots and a smile line could be compelling. Once I had seen her face, I didn't ever want to lose her.

Nannie began to talk with animation about Mary's new activities. 'She likes paper. She loves to shake and rattle paper and plastic bags.' Nannie gave Mary a small one. We smiled as we watched Mary wildly waving it around, laughing as she made it crackle.

'Has she rolled over yet?' I asked.

'No, but sometimes she nearly does.'

The other two came tumbling into the room. Bonnie jumped on to the bed one side of Mary, and Mark sprawled himself on the other. Mary tightened up as they tickled her. She laughed with them as they began singing:

Mary, Mary, give me your answer, do!
I'm half crazy all for the love of you . . .

I'd always delighted in seeing the three of them together, my sturdy pink-cheeked flower-fresh sparkling-eyed children. They were my treasures, I'd tell them, my three jewels.

'What if somebody gave you a million dollars?' Mark would ask. 'Then would you sell us?'

'Oh, no,' I'd say, my voice very serious, pretending to be horrified.

'Would you sell just one?'

'Never!'

'What about for a billion?'

'Not even a billion. Or a trillion.' I would shake my head sorrowfully.

'A zillion?'

'No, you're much too precious.'

'Infinity precious?' Mark had become fascinated by the idea of infinity – he often used it as an adverb, fashioning his own compounds: infinity-sweet, infinity-ugly, infinity-nice.

'Oh, yes, Mark. Infinity precious.'

Shock

When I came out of Mary's room Marlene was hovering in the dark hallway. She frowned and tugged at her sweater sleeves, first one and then the other.

'Dr Webb stopped in to see Mary when he came to look at Mark's throat.'

'That was thoughtful of him,' I said lightly. Dr Niall Webb, whose office was in his home up the hill, at the top of the street, always asked about Mary. He would peek in to see her whenever he made a call at the house. 'Was she asleep or crying when he came this time?'

'Neither.'

'Good!'

Marlene studied her overlong fingernails.

'He said that he wanted to see you as soon as you came back.'

'Wanted to see me?'

'Yes.'

'Mary?'

'Yes.'

'Why?'

'Ask Nannie.'

'Oh!'

Marlene still wasn't looking at me.

I went back into Mary's room. The older children had left and Nannie had turned out the light so that Mary could sleep.

'Marlene said that Dr Webb wanted to see me . . .'

Nannie didn't look at me directly. In the semi-darkness her eyes were hooded.

'Oh, yes. When he came to see Mark, he looked in here . . .'

'Did he examine her?'

'Oh, no! Nothing like that. Just put his head in for a moment, as he always does.'

'And she was awake?'

'Yes. She was smiling at him.'

'But what happened?'

'Nothing.' Nannie's voice was low and she was looking down, fussing with the tassles on the bedspread. Suddenly she burst out – guiltily, almost angrily. 'There is nothing I can tell you. He didn't tell me anything.'

Something was horribly wrong.

'Dr Webb's office hours begin at two,' I said, and stood up, looking at the baby. 'I'll go see him at two.'

I hurried up the hill towards the house, fronting Burdett Avenue on the main Dalkey road, where the doctor's office was. Months earlier Dr Webb had responded instantly when I'd called him about Bonnie, who was suffering what I thought was severe constipation. He'd come to the house immediately. He'd diagnosed the real problem – acute appendicitis – and had her rushed to the hospital for emergency surgery. Dr Webb's availability had probably saved her life. And he'd had me rushed to the hospital the day I went to him for a prenatal check-up – and haemorrhaged in his office. I had reason to be grateful to this immensely competent man.

The tall door opened into a narrow hallway. I entered an anteroom on the right where Dr Webb's secretary sat. I gave her my name and she pulled our file. I went over to sit down in one of the carved wooden chairs.

Though it was just after two, a number of other people

were in the room sitting quietly or reading. There were many chairs and leather couches in the high-ceilinged room. Lamps glowed, fashioning yellow auras of cheer in the dimness of grey light that filtered through the venetian blinds.

What was it the doctor wanted to tell me?

In a half-dream the day after Mary was born, before she'd had a name, I'd imagined an infant's voice announcing its departure. *Well, I must go along now; it's time.*

Oh, no! Please stay, I'd said. *Please! You can't go now, we don't want you to go away.*

Dr Webb emerged from his office, said good-bye to a patient, returned the folder and took another one from his secretary. He did this several times, whispering a name into the big room, bowing tentatively and ushering in another patient. Finally he came out and called my name. He seemed a little abashed. The Irish had that way of looking as though they'd been caught at something, and they'd smile even when there was nothing to smile about. It was a charming quality, but at this moment his smile only made me uncomfortable. 'Ah,' he said, as we sat down inside his office, 'Mrs Collins. I just wanted to talk to you for a moment. When I looked in on Mary – ' he frowned in an effort to find the words – 'her face, it didn't look right.'

'In what way?'

'Well,' he coughed and shifted his weight. 'There are no worry lines.'

I felt he was struggling to say what he meant without saying too much.

'Her eyes, you know. They put one off a bit – '

I interrupted him, rising to Mary's defence, recounting her little achievements over the last several months. 'Yes, it's true Mary's eyes are slightly unbalanced. I had that problem as a child. But now I'm fine.' I stared at him, not

15

really seeing, as I thought wildly of other ways to deny his accusation. But I'd already admitted some of the truth. There'd been that moment in Mary's room when Nannie could tell me nothing.

'Perhaps,' I said, urging the words out, 'we gave her too much of the colic medicine. Nannie might have given her too much.' It was not a way of blaming Nannie but of blaming myself. I'd given Nannie so much of the responsibility.

'No, I don't think so – '

He was shaking his head, drawing in his breath, searching for the right words. He meant – he had to mean – that Mary was retarded. It was the worst thing I could think of. It was the only thing I could think of. I interrupted him again.

'She just has a lot of catching up to do. She was so premature. And then she had that colic.'

I was pleading now.

'No, Mrs Collins. I think she has cerebral palsy.'

I bent over and put my face in my hands. I wanted the doctor to vanish. What he'd said – I wanted it erased. I turned away from this new reality looming towards me. I felt I couldn't breathe.

'I know,' he said. 'It's hard, very hard.' Dr Webb's face was kind. His eyes revealed his distress.

Cerebral palsy. What did that mean? A horrible paralysis of some kind. That's what the word palsy meant. He couldn't possibly be talking about Mary – innocent little Mary with her oval face and rosebud mouth, who was going to grow up to be a lovely, graceful girl like her sister Bonnie. There must be some mistake, I thought. I didn't see how he could be so certain as all that. Not yet.

He took his prescription pad and tore off a leaf. He wrote down a name and said, 'This is the director of the Central Remedial Clinic. I'll call him and ask that they see Mary as soon as possible. But you'll have to phone and set up the appointment.' I took the piece of paper, as he was saying, 'It's a bit far from here – Clontarf. It's in north Dublin. But they're very good there.' Sandycove was a southern suburb. Clontarf was the other side of the moon as far as I was concerned.

'The clinic there is the best in Ireland,' he said, standing up and leading me through the door of his office, then through the little hallway. He opened the front door for me. I mumbled my rote thank you's, left the building, and closed the door. Below me were the dozen or so stone steps that led down to the front gate. From this height I looked straight into the sky above the Irish Sea. I descended the steps, and crossed the road.

Heavily, I began to walk down the hill.

What Had I Done?

The air that afternoon in early March was cold and smelled of the sea. I continued walking down the hill. The street was empty of people. I heard a hubbub of inner voices, though, getting louder, echoing what the doctor had told me. I heard myself answering that I didn't want this, no, no, no. At the foot of the hill the house looked forlorn. As I came to the green wooden gate, pushing up on its rusty latch, I saw the little garden, full of dead weeds and dry twigs. The sea was at low tide, revealing a bottom of stone and slime, the bed barren and brown for a long way out. It was a wasteland – wet and scummy and strange, giving off a dank odour. Tom, I thought, never sees it at these times; or if he does, he doesn't pay attention. Probably he only really notices it when the tide is high and the sky bright, when the blue rippling water, mirroring white clouds, floods up against the seawall. I wondered whether I should call Tom now. It would be about ten in the morning in New York. I wanted to hear his voice, hear him deny that there was anything wrong with Mary, or at least say that cerebral palsy was less serious than I thought. I decided to wait for the lower rate, to call him in the evening.

Indoors, it seemed odd that everything was going on normally. Nannie walked into the kitchen, holding Mary in that special way she had – her left forearm supporting Mary's stomach and the familiar cloth draped over her left shoulder.

Nannie looked tense and anxious.

I said it bluntly. 'Mary has cerebral palsy. We have to take her to a clinic in Clontarf.' Mary's little face turned up to me as she heard my voice. Nannie sat down, looked at me and sighed, shaking her head and stroking Mary's back. Seeing the sorrow in Nannie's eyes, I took Mary from her and sat down myself in the little dining area. Nannie fell into a chair and was squeezing her hands in her lap. She looked utterly grief stricken.

'What did he tell you? Dr Webb, I mean?'

'Her face,' I began, looking at Mary, who was smiling. With her right hand she was shaking some plastic discs on a metal chain. *She hardly ever uses her left hand,* I realised with some shock. I was beginning to see.

'He said she doesn't have any worry lines.' I hesitated. Nannie looked terribly distraught. 'I guess,' I said, 'we'll just have to find out exactly what the problem is.'

Nannie nodded mournfully. 'At the hospital they wanted to see her again.'

A month ago, although I'd been home, Nannie had taken Mary to the maternity hospital at Holles Street for the regular bi-monthly checkup required for babies born prematurely. That day I'd been busy getting ready to fly to New York. I recalled Nannie returning from the hospital, bundling Mary into her room and closing the door. I'd been busy packing my portfolios and a suitcase, and had left shortly afterwards with hurried good-byes.

'I didn't want to worry you,' Nannie was saying.

'What do you mean?'

'Dr O'Brien, at the hospital, said something about her stiffness. He said it wasn't normal. Something wasn't right, he said. But he wouldn't tell me anything more. He said to have the mother bring the child down at the next appointment. I didn't want to mention it to you before you left. I mean there was nothing definite I could have told you anyway.'

'I guess it *was* better not to tell me, Nannie. I'm glad you didn't.' I could never have gone to New York, could not have mustered enthusiasm for all the layout work, for the hours and days of planning and measuring and pasting. Not if I'd been aware little Mary was in difficulty. 'You were right not to mention it, Nannie.'

Marlene walked in. I gathered from her face she'd heard some of the conversation.

'Hi, Mary!' she said. Then, to Nannie and me, 'I'll get us some coffee, okay?' She put the kettle on, then returned and sat down.

'Dr Webb thinks Mary has cerebral palsy,' I said. 'I'll have to bring her to a clinic to be examined.'

'When?' Marlene asked.

'I have to call.'

'You'll be all right, Mary,' Marlene said softly to the baby. As the kettle hummed, she turned to the kitchen. Presently she reappeared, carrying the stainless steel pot of fresh coffee and the pint-size creamer filled with hot milk. Marlene had lived in Switzerland for two years and this *café au lait* was her speciality. As she was pouring, Bonnie and Mark came bouncing in with cries of 'Mary! Mary!' As soon as the baby saw Bonnie she wanted to go to her. Bonnie picked Mary up, adjusting her in her arms, efficiently patting the blanket around her, getting her comfortable. Then Bonnie did a little up and down dance, making Mary laugh and squeal. I saw Mary's face, over Bonnie's shoulder, brighten with pleasure. Mark darted at Mary, making quick jabs at her. The baby shrieked with delight.

Then Bonnie whirled around and thrust Mary back at me. 'Here she is, Mommy. Mary is a *good* girl! Mary, see Mommie?' Mary, suddenly realising that she was being peremptorily deposited, that there would be no further entertainment from Bonnie and Mark, began to fret, her lip quivering. The older children, sensing the emergency, jumped up and down for her, singing, 'Waltzing Matilda'. Mary relaxed in my arms and listened to the singing.

'You shouldn't pick her up like that, and then just go off and leave her –' Nannie began, in a tired voice.

'Mary's okay now,' Bonnie crooned for the baby's benefit. 'Aren't you, Mary? Do you see Nannie?' Bonnie cocked her head at Mary, then went whisking out of the room, followed by Mark. Nannie was right. Often Bonnie managed to calm Mary when none of the rest of us could. But often too, just when Nannie had got a fussy colicky baby relaxed and sleepy, Bonnie would skip in, jiggle Mary around, and then fly off to other pursuits, leaving Nannie in the lurch.

It was quiet in the room again. Mary was energetically batting the arm of my chair.

'I just can't believe it,' I said. 'About Mary.'

'I know,' Nannie sighed.

Marlene sat there stirring her coffee. It was growing dark. I got up with Mary and went into the kitchen. Marlene had already started supper. Holding Mary, I studied her closely. She stared up at me, one eye wandering off. As she noticed how intent I was, her mouth, below the tiny nose set between fat cheeks, curved in a smile. She *was* stiff, so stiff that her body seemed all of a piece. I held her under the arms; her legs stretched straight out. Cerebral palsy? What did that mean? Did it mean she would never walk?

All I knew for certain was that the child I thought I'd borne had been taken away from me.

That night I placed the transatlantic call to Tom, and went to the couch in the sitting-room. Waiting for the operator to ring back, I sat there for ten, fifteen, twenty minutes. What had I done? Suddenly with wild force came the chilling realisation that, ten months ago, trying to finish some work before we left New York to move to Ireland, I'd been so anxious to avoid an all-day round trip from New Jersey to New York that I'd missed my May prenatal checkup. I knew enough about pregnancy, I told myself then, to be able to detect signs of problems. I'd had two healthy children. I'd read so many books about pregnancy. I'd been a natural childbirth enthusiast. I'd stopped smoking. I rarely had anything to drink. I was careful to eat well and to rest often. I took the prescribed huge purple vitamin pill every day, and felt fine. So I'd decided to skip the trip. In Dublin I'd have to find a new doctor anyway.

Yet I hadn't anticipated what would happen when we arrived in Sandycove – Bonnie's sudden appendicitis, the trips to visit her every day in the children's hospital. I kept intending to make an appointment with a gynaecologist, but the days rushed by. There was the work I was setting up, and the interviews with prospective staff . . .

If only I'd seen a doctor before leaving America! If only I'd seen a doctor as soon as I'd arrived in Ireland! It was my own fault. Little Mary! If only I hadn't gone along with Tom's move!

Struggling to remain rational, I reminded myself that it had been a *placenta praevia* condition, impossible to diagnose as early as May. Even in the hospital they'd needed all their sophisticated equipment to tell what was going wrong. So the condition had *not* been the result of my failure to see a doctor in May – I must remember that.

But maybe, I thought again, I *could* have prevented it. Maybe, somehow, the condition could have been diagnosed, and I'd have been told to go to bed and stay there.

What had I done? What had I done to my own child?

I gave a start when I heard the staccato ring-ring, ring-ring, ring-ring. I picked up the phone.

'Go ahead now, please,' said the operator.

As soon as I heard his voice I said, all in one breath: 'Oh, Tom, Mary's retarded. I took her to the doctor and he said she has cerebral palsy!'

'What happened? Mary? Retarded? How do you know?' His voice was muffled and came to me as a kind of stutter. At five-thirty in the evening, in the middle of some problem in the office, he would not be expecting a call from Ireland. 'Pat, tell me slowly. What is it?'

'Mary has cerebral palsy. Dr Webb said so. Remember the breathing difficulty she had after she was born? That probably caused it. And she was just born too soon!'

'Oh! Poor little Mary. She was doing so well.'

'They want to examine her at a clinic where they take infants. Dr Webb didn't say much. Only that her face didn't look right. Bland. No worry lines. Her eyes – just by looking at her eyes he could tell something was wrong. And I never even noticed anything!'

'I don't get it.'

'Dr Webb saw Mary while I was away then told them at the house here that I was to see him when I returned. So I saw him. Today, this afternoon. Oh, Tom, what are we going to do?'

'Well, Pat, we'll just have to see what they say at the clinic.'

'Did you ever think anything was wrong with Mary?'

'No.'

'I can't believe it.'

'Maybe it's not so bad. My cousin Bill had cerebral palsy. Spastic on one side. But he could pass a football. And was very good at basketball. Very bright, too. A great comic – '

'But not Mary! Our little Mary!' I was angry with Tom.

'Mary will be okay, Pat. See what the other doctor has to say. You don't know anything for certain. Maybe she's

23

really okay. Or maybe it won't turn out to be so serious after all.'

That was what I wanted to hear, what I had called to hear Tom say. But somehow it made me even angrier.

'Tom, maybe she won't be okay. Maybe we did this to her, by just not taking enough *care*.'

'What?'

'If we hadn't come to this place – left everything and come over here, with all our problems. It was stupid. I let this happen. If I hadn't taken on so much, Mary wouldn't have been premature.'

'No, Pat. Don't!' Tom paused, stopped, sighed. Whenever he was under pressure he would become very quiet. His words would be measured and carefully chosen.

'When are you going to take Mary to the other doctor?'

'I don't know yet. Probably next week.' It was a struggle to think beyond the moment.

'Well, we really won't know anything definite till then. Right?'

'But I know Mary has something wrong with her. *Now*. And *we* did this to her!'

'Pat!'

'We yanked ourselves right out of a good and normal situation at home and came here. Never minding that I was five months pregnant. Never minding anything except doing it. We weren't ready. How could I have done such a thing? I can't stand it. I can't *stand* myself.'

'But you know you're putting this on my shoulders.'

'I'm blaming *myself*,' I shouted, 'I hate myself.' I knew he was right, but I was pounding the table with my fist, my eyes shut, my voice loud, my rage running free. 'We didn't think. Either of us. We should have taken more *care*. It's too late now. I don't mind the projects going sour. But I can't take this. I just can't.'

'Pull yourself together, Pat.'

'Pull myself together?' I shrieked. 'What *for*? Don't you see what I've done? To an innocent baby, my own child?'

'You've got to *stop* thinking that way!'

'I can't help it. I can't get it out of my mind.' I was ready to cry.

'Do you want me to come over?'

'No!' I knew there was too much happening in New York. 'It'll only make things worse. The books you're working on – there'll only be more problems if you come over. Besides – what could you do? Nothing that would make Mary be normal again. You're not a magician – ' I began to wind up again, as Tom interrupted.

'I will come over. I'll get a plane tomorrow night. I'll be in Sandycove Wednesday morning.'

'Are you sure? I *would* like to see you!' I was finally beginning to realise what I had been doing to Tom's feelings. 'I'm sorry. But – little Mary! It breaks my heart.'

'We'll figure it out together.' Tom's voice was uncertain but his tone was warm and kind; I had counted on this. I felt ashamed. After we hung up, I stared at the reflected light in the panes of the upstairs sitting-room window. It was very quiet. Mary, often awake at this time and crying fitfully, was asleep. But I felt no peace at all. My mind leapt all over the landscape: Mary downstairs, Mary's weeks in the hospital, Mary going to the doctor at the clinic. What would he say? What really was cerebral palsy? New methods – so much could be done today. How seriously was Mary affected? I imagined Mary at ten, at eighteen. Not as I'd been imagining her all these months – oh, no! I saw her limping, saw her head shaking as she tried to talk, heard the halting words coming out. Tears burned my eyes. I put my head in my hands and cried.

A Changeling

When I went to bed I couldn't sleep. The gleam of a street lamp shone in the window, casting a tree's flickering shadows on the wall of the bedroom. Familiar images of the future, of what had been the future, paraded by. Mary wearing clothes I'd put away for her; Mary in school; Mary running with Bonnie and Mark; Mary as a teenager; Mary as a young woman. I'd always thought of Mary as a happy, robust, bright-eyed, intelligent girl! I'd never thought about her in any other way. The Mary I'd conceived in my mind was as real to me as the Mary sleeping now in the bedroom downstairs. I'd studied her face carefully, discovering which of the family she most closely resembled. I'd decided how she would look as she grew older. I'd compared her with Bonnie and Mark, projected qualities of personality on to the emergent Mary of the future. I'd formed a very definite idea of Mary, very real to me. Now she was gone. Never to be. Mary had been taken away from me, and this other child put in her place: a changeling.

One day months ago, when Mary was several weeks old, Tom and I had gone to the Holles Street hospital to see her. A Dr Niall O'Brien was in charge of the sixth floor infants' intensive care ward. We had questions and everybody at the hospital said Dr O'Brien was the expert. So we sought him out, finally catching up with him in a hallway. He spoke briskly, even curtly, with the air of someone who could only be stopped briefly on his way to some urgent appointment. Tom asked if Mary would be all right. Was she out of danger? Tom wanted to know.

'Yes, yes,' Dr O'Brien said with a frown. 'She seems to be doing very well. She eats a lot and is gaining weight, and appears to be quite strong.' He stared at us impatiently.

'Well,' Tom went on, not knowing quite what it was he was asking. 'Will she be normal? Will she, you know, be able to do things?'

Dr. O'Brien paused. Looking away from us towards the direction of the nursery, he said 'It's just too early to tell. There's nothing to be said definitely. She seems to have done well so far.'

'Of course!' I broke in, anxious to have Tom stop asking questions, anxious to placate the busy doctor. For me it was enough that she was all right now.

The day Mary was born the head nurse had warned me. 'She's not three and a half pounds yet. She may not survive. You mustn't count on it.' But Mary was sealed into an incubator, an intravenous tube attached to her umbilical, and during her first twenty-four hours she didn't weaken or become still. An oxygen funnel was placed on the white mattress in front of her tiny face. So when she lived through that first day, and didn't disappear or go away, I was certain that she would survive, that she would come to enjoy the fulness of life.

But, after her initial difficulty, in the hands of Dr O'Brien and his staff she was developing nicely. Why was Tom insisting on questioning her future? Other women had lost their premature babies; mine was alive, and thriving. Oh, perhaps she would need glasses, or would not be perfectly co-ordinated, or would be a little slow in school. Because of her premature birth, I fully accepted the possibility of small diminishments. 'It's just too early to tell,' I said, repeating the doctor's words to Tom. Tom nodded, accepting my wish that the conversation be ended. Without another word Dr O'Brien pushed through the swinging doors towards the ward, his white coat flapping in his own breeze.

Lying restless in bed I asked how I had managed to miss the signs. Had Nannie been hiding something from me? Had I been hiding something from myself? *Isn't she a big girl, Mommy?* Bonnie, sitting on Mary's bed, her back against the wall, had asked me this morning, reaching for Mary, lifting her to a sitting position on her lap. Mary had turned her head up, eyes fixed on her big sister. No, not fixed. Mary's left eye wandered off a bit – a weak muscle, I'd thought. Mary had trouble focusing both eyes together! This morning, too, Mark had said something strange. He'd put his forefinger into Mary's palm, and she'd given him a wide smile. *I like the feel of it when she holds on real tight*, Mark had said. Mary had trouble relaxing her grip! Suddenly I recalled Marlene questioning me, more than once. *When Bonnie was a baby, when did she begin to sit up? When did Mark begin to talk?* and Marlene had seemed so eager to tell me of her mother's letters about her brother when he was a baby – all the mischief he'd got into before he was a year old. Had I myself suspected something all along? *Has she rolled over yet?* I'd asked this morning.

I remembered how abrupt it had seemed when, after Mary had spent just seven weeks in the hospital, I was told I could take the tiny infant home. Nannie was away, taking a much needed month's rest, visiting her family in Roscommon. That first night I'd kept Mary in my room, in a makeshift bed next to my own. I'd been terribly worried that she would find some way to die. *(Well, I must go along now. It's time.)* The covers would tangle around her and suffocate her, or she would spit up and choke, or she would simply stop breathing. I fed her twice that first night. I set the clock on the edge of the night table, and checked her every half hour. In the morning I felt new awe at the power of her frail presence, her fast-beating heart, her fingers curling tightly – like bird's claws – around my large finger. The miracle child, it was August and she was seven weeks old, yet her birth shouldn't have come till September.

She cried fitfully that night. The following day, Nannie returned from Roscommon and eagerly took over caring for Mary. I was relieved to let her swaddle Mary in blankets, let her worry about the temperature of the room, let her check how many ounces of milk Mary consumed. Nannie could pat Mary's back and rock her to sleep. And I could return again to the problem of the filmstrips, which with all the static from the American editor had begun to fall dangerously behind schedule.

Now I was lying here, and the Mary downstairs was not the Mary I'd come to know in the months since. In folktales, a mother goes to sleep one night leaving her infant unprotected. Beings from the faery world steal in and kidnap the infant from its cradle, substituting a faery child. Though this changeling resembles the human child, the mother knows it is different. This is what had happened to me. I shook my head back and forth on the pillow. Where, oh where, was the other Mary? Why had she been taken away? She would never take her place with Mark and Bonnie, nor with any laughing, running, jumping children – she would always be different, maybe very different. The Mary I had known had vanished:

A reed that grows never more again
As a reed among reeds in the river . . .

Nightmare

The dark in the quiet room, though heavy, seemed filled with a certain presence – as though in a hushed theatre the curtain had gone up on a darkened stage. There was nothing happening. Yet some kind of presence hovered in the room and in the house that night.

I woke at three in the morning, dreaming I had been in a makeshift, added-on, whitewalled kitchen like the one in Sandycove. There was a chair against the wall near the stove, and Mary, suddenly three years old, was standing on the chair. Somebody was stirring something in a pot. 'Bonnie, Bonnie Collins,' Mary was singing, dipping up and down as she sang. Her face flushed from the heat of the stove, Mary had damp curls all round her head. Bonnie at that age had looked like that. So had Mark. There was a fresh happiness about the image, reassuring in its very ordinariness. Then I woke fully to the nightmare realisation that Mary would never stand on a chair and sing like that. Mary was not that Mary anymore, but another Mary. This terrified me. (What is there about three o'clock in the morning that tinges everything with dread?) I lay there tormented, wishing it were daybreak. My body was clammy. I found it difficult to breathe.

Still grieving for the child that had gone, I fell asleep and dreamed another dream: There was a large picnic area near a stream in a forest. People who had worked with Tom and me were there, eating and talking animatedly among themselves. I was approaching with a wooden cart

– a platform supported with small wooden wheels. I pushed the cart with a long waist-high crossbar. Bonnie and Mark were walking along guiltily beside me. In the cart was a grotesquely twisted Mary, lying so stiffly on the platform that I was sure she would fall off. At length we reached the picnic area. The people there were silent as they stared at Mary. Finally one man came over to the cart and stood there, his unbelieving eyes fixed on Mary's deformed body, shaking his head. See what you've done! his look and gesture said.

I woke again, relieved. Mary was not lying in a cart all twisted and misshapen. She was safely in her bed downstairs. Then I recognised the image. It was from the cart used to wheel helpless children around the infamous New York asylum, Willowbrook. I'd seen it in a magazine: a cart whose sides were no more than five or six inches above the ground, and in it an emaciated and nearly naked girl of seven, who had been left lying alone for hours. Willowbrook meant then an institution where children were left unattended, victims of bad food, bedsores, neglect. One helpless child there had been burned to death in a scalding hot shower.

Suddenly I heard loud cries. Mary – she was still waking up at night. Would this be one of her long crying sessions? Should I go down? Nannie had never been able to get her to follow a definite schedule. Nannie and I both thought of Mary as being delicate; so we'd get her to take as much food as she could. Nannie, in her random purposeful way, followed Mary around the clock. She'd get her to sleep, feed her when she woke, then get her off to sleep again as soon as possible.

A few months ago there had been a long series of bad nights, when Nannie would walk with her, or I'd put her on my shoulder and stroke her back – anything to get her to sleep. Sometimes nothing would work. Tears would squeeze from her eyes, wetting her face; she'd cry and cry, her face becoming burnt and fiery. Her clothes would always be damp with sweat. When the screaming would stop and I'd feel her relax a bit, I'd lay her in the carriage, half on her side, and Nannie would wad diapers and crib blankets around her. 'It makes her feel more secure,' she'd say. 'She needs the comfort.' One of us would rub the child's back. Wet and exhausted, she'd finally fall asleep. This continued for weeks.

After one very long night, when Mary's screams persisted into the morning, I'd phoned Dr Webb. He agreed to stop off on his daily rounds and examine her. When he arrived Mary was crying. He put his hands on her abdomen. Stroking her head, he said simply, 'It's gas. Colic.' Nannie sighed profoundly. 'Oh, just gas,' she said. 'But she seems in such pain,' I said. 'Colic can be terribly painful,' the doctor said. 'Sometimes, for gas, I've had to give grown men morphine.' He wrote out a prescription for a sedative to put in her milk. As he left he said, 'Don't worry. She'll grow out of it eventually.'

Though in time the colic would become less severe, the pattern would continue. At night Mary would wake and cry; Nannie would feed her and walk with her until she slept again. In the morning when I'd go in to her, Mary would be asleep. And then she'd sleep again later in the day.

Tonight as I lay listening, her crying grew softer and finally subsided. I turned over and fell into a deep sleep. In the morning I woke to running footsteps in the hallway. The mantel in the bedroom caught a beam of sunlight. The green tile around the fireplace sparkled. The clock said seven. I blinked my eyes and tried to remember what day it was. I felt a vague unease. Then, as though a gear shifted in my stomach, I recalled Mary's bland face, her wandering eyes, her stiff body. She couldn't work her arms and legs as a normal child could. Then came the icy realisation.

Mary was handicapped; retarded in some way.

Oh, my God!

Reproach

I threw off the covers and stood up. I had to have something to wear. I found a sweater and skirt and put them on. I pulled the bed together, opened the bedroom door and stepped out into the hallway. To the left was the sitting-room. To the right and down four steps was the little room where Marlene used to sleep before she took an apartment in nearby Dalkey. Now Mark slept there, pleased with his privacy and the fact that a television set was kept in a corner there.

Just then he emerged from the room.

'Hi, Mommy: Bonnie's upstairs. Mary's awake in the kitchen with Nannie.' Having announced everyone's whereabouts, he proceeded to discuss the order of the day. Mark had a habit of schematising. Taking my hand as we went downstairs, he said, 'You have your coffee and we'll eat breakfast. Nannie already had her coffee. Bonnie had eggs with Nannie. Bonnie's getting dressed and she's hurrying to get the bus. Will you walk to Miss Murray's with me? Are you going out today? Will you be back to pick me up?'

Miss Murray ran a nursery school, a short three blocks away, in a house near Sandycove Harbour. A huge table filled the centre of an upstairs room; around the table near the walls were little desks. It was here that Mark was learning lettering, counting and colouring. Here too, he learned prayers and heard hair-raising stories about devils and hell.

'Yes.' I smiled at Mark. Even if I wanted to say no, it was

34

always best to find a way to couch everything in the affirmative for this very emotional child. His feelings always surfaced on his face, passing like fleeting clouds, from anger despair to joy, from sorrow to gladness.

'Daddy's coming today.'

He looked up, his eyes wide. 'When?'

'He'll be here when you come home from school.'

'Will he bring me something, too?'

'Maybe. Is your bad sore throat all better?'

'Well, it feels good now.' Touching his throat gingerly, he opened and shut his mouth. 'Dr Webb fixed it.'

'Good!'

'But it might get bad again today,' he added darkly.

That morning I worked near the front window of the second floor office, listening to the cars as they chugged along the searoad and putted up Burdette Avenue. Usually the plane from New York landed about nine-thirty; an hour or so later Tom would arrive with his briefcase and small overnight bag. In his frequent trips he'd become quite an expert packer and had pared his luggage down to a few essentials.

After several false arrivals, I heard what I knew was a taxi motor droning in the street below. I heard doors opening and slamming. Coffee cup in hand, I sped to the bay window over the desk table and looked out through the sheer patterned curtains. There was Tom, busily counting out bills and coins. The two bags were on the ground, and Tom's overcoat bulged around the suit jacket pockets, where he kept all his tickets, notepads, pens, wallet and namecards. He had a neatly folded newspaper under his arm.

The driver bobbed up and down, and then, the transaction completed, disappeared into his taxi and drove off. I tapped on the window and Tom looked up and waved. I could see that he was very pale and had dark circles around his eyes. The trip – he hadn't had much chance to sleep. His hair trimmed short, he looked very boyish. He always looked boyish, with his long-lashed blue eyes and quick smile. His gestures were quick and definite. He seemed to work from extraordinary reserves of energy. There was usually a spring to his step but now, as I watched him, he bent over slowly to pick up his small bags. Stooping slightly, his head down, he leaned forward and pushed open the green gate.

I ran from the window through the room to the hall. I clattered down the stairs to the hall and flung open the door.

'Oh, Tom, I'm so glad you came! Thank you for coming.' I hugged him, bags and all. He seemed so quiet and slow. I looked at his face.

'Are you tired?'

'I don't know. But, Pat, after all – that phone call of yours – ' He looked at me reproachfully.

I had expected Tom to spread the blanket of his warm goodwill and soothing calm over me like a mantle. Instead he was tired and upset, a creature of my anxiety.

'I'm so sorry. I didn't think, I didn't mean to get you into a state, too.' I wanted Tom happy, wanted him to talk about Mary and say that everything was really all right.

He was my support, and he was crumbling before me.

'What did you think would happen?' He shook his head. 'Anyway, I've decided that since I'm over here, I'll go on to London. After we've had a good talk. The day after tomorrow.'

'The day after tomorrow?'

'Don't worry,' he said. 'It'll all work out.'

'It'll all work out? Do you mean your meeting in London? Or the projects? Or Mary's problem?' A new wave of emotion was gathering in me. 'Things will all work out? Look how they've already worked out! Things don't work out. They just *don't*, sometimes.'

'Pat, it saved Bonnie's life, being here. The appendicitis –'

'Maybe it did. I don't know. All I know is that Mary is destroyed, and it's our fault, my fault.'

He didn't say anything then. Standing there, I leaned over to pick up one of the bags. Realising all the pain we shared, I suddenly saw us as a sort of four-legged Job. Job with his sores, with his family taken from him, with the contempt of his friends.

'Where's Mary now?' Tom asked.

'In with Nannie. She'll be awake. Do you want to see her?'

We went into the house, put the bags aside, and walked together down the hallway to the little white room with Nannie's bed and Mary's empty crib in it. Mary was lying on the bed, the blankets and pillows around her. She smiled when she saw us. Nannie had been sitting on the edge of the bed reading a newspaper. Now she stood up and went over to Mary and began to fix her clothing.

'Daddy's here, Mary,' Nannie said. 'He came to see you!' She smoothed Mary's wisps of hair and began to button the snaps on the front of her little cloth jumpsuit.

Tom, his coat still on, went over to Mary. The bed was low and Tom knelt down, bringing his face close to hers. He spoke softly to her as always.

'Hi, there, Mary!' he said. As he talked she waved her right arm, her right leg jabbing at his sleeve. He grabbed her foot and shook it up and down. He cocked his head to the side and made Donald Duck sounds. Mary loved it, as the other children did.

'She looks fine to me,' Tom said, a little defiantly. Nannie's eyes lighted, feeding on the defiance.

'Oh, she's a good, good girl!' she said, leaning towards Mary and stroking her tummy.

'Sure, she is.' Tom stood up and folded his arms. He studied Mary intently. Seeing her still gazing at him, he tilted his head again and made more duck noises. He made a quick little jump away. 'See you later,' he squawked in the duck voice. She squealed, and he waved to her as he backed from the room. 'Bye-bye for now, Mary! Bye-bye!'

We closed the door behind us and walked over towards the kitchen doorway.

'Do you want something to eat?' I asked.

'No, thanks. I think I'll sleep now,' he said. 'We can talk later.'

We climbed the stairs. Tom, exhausted, was soon fast asleep in the darkened bedroom, his coat and suit hung neatly in the wardrobe, his bags unopened on the floor.

It was mid-afternoon of the same day.

'You have to leave again so soon?' I asked Tom.

'For a few days. I'll go to London first. And then maybe on to Paris.' We had some French editors, friends of ours, who were working for us there on a freelance basis.

The children, just returned from school, entered the dark bedroom, noisily greeting Tom. Bonnie began busily rubbing his back. He sat on the edge of the bed, his elbows resting on his knees, his hands clasped together. He smiled at Mark, silent now after an explosion of chatter and solemnly staring at his father.

'If only there was something *definite*,' I said. One of Tom's strengths was his ability to gather people together and make something happen – a book project, an educational package with a blue-ribbon editorial board to support it. He had done it in New York dozens of times. His enthusiasm was contagious, and his genuine delight in people's talents, skills or scholarship won him co-operation from even the surliest creative types. He was *very* persuasive. But at the moment his magic wasn't working, hadn't in fact been working for several months now, since a temperamental author had once again reneged on his promise, costing us tens of thousands of dollars and creating problems with disappointed publishers. We were going into debt, and it seemed to me that at this point Tom's attempts to move things along were so much wheel-spinning.

The children went bobbing and skipping out of the room. I heard them bouncing down the stairs, their cheerful voices carrying through the house. Tom still sat on the edge of the bed.

'I hope you're not throwing good money after bad,' I said.

'What do you mean, Pat? I'm doing the best I can.'

'I wouldn't mind all this trouble with the business,' I said, 'if only Mary were all right. I can't stand thinking that she's not.'

It was so quiet in the room that we seemed caught in a parenthesis of time. No one was pressing for our attention; nothing had to be taken care of in a rush. It was oddly peaceful. Tom didn't speak at all for a while. Then he sighed, and sat up straight, putting his hands on his knees.

'Well,' he said in a slow bemused way, as though seeing something for the first time. 'It will be interesting to see how Mary develops.'

'Interesting? Good God, Tom! Is that all you think?'

'We don't have much to go on yet.'

'You don't seem – well, Tom, you just don't seem very concerned about her future.'

'But I am. Of course I am. I can't say that I'm worried, though. Sure, she may not be able to walk. But she may turn out to be very intelligent.'

'You're saying that because that's what you'd *like* to

think. It's easier for you. Tom, you're too optimistic – about everything!'

'Maybe. But Pat, all you know about Mary is what Dr Webb told you. The rest of it, well, you're cooking it up in your head.'

'It's not just in my head! I can see – '

'What is it you see?'

'Mary! Her face, her eyes. She can't do things she should be able to do – '

'You don't know, Pat. You really don't know anything yet.'

'Well, I soon will. I'm seeing the doctors next week. And you'll be gone. You'll be in Europe.'

'Yes,' he admitted. 'But I'll be back here afterwards.'

Tom leaned forward and took my hand, tugging me over so that I'd sit next to him. I did, and he put his arms around me.

The Verdict

Monday, after I'd taken Mark to Miss Murray's, I phoned the taxi rank at Dun Laoghaire. Tom had left for London three days earlier, after an elaborate good-bye to Mary. I was going to see the same Dr O'Brien whom Tom had questioned seven months ago about Mary's chances for normal development. Now, so long afterwards, some kind of answer would be given.

A taxi came. It was the slow driver, the one we always tried to avoid. Nannie fussed with Mary's blankets, loosening them here, tightening there, as we made our way down the pebble path and through the gate. The driver stood solemnly beside the open door. My arms locked around Mary, I hitched myself into the back seat. Nannie followed me into the cab, tucking away at Mary's blankets. The door closed, Nannie eyed her handiwork critically, jabbing at Mary's scarf, frowning at a fold. Finally settling herself into the seat, she bent forward, smiling and nodding. 'Mary is going bye-bye in a taxi,' she said in a hoarse whisper. Mary peered up from the blankets and grinned at Nannie, her body stiffening with excitement. In a large navy bag at Nannie's feet were bottles of milk and juice, paper diapers, soft cloths, pacifiers; all the impedimenta she thought necessary to meet the hazards of a journey beyond the warm safe walls of home.

'Maybe she'll sleep a little,' Nannie said. She believed with all her heart that sleeping cured all infant ills.

Mary was making fretting noises as Nannie bent forward, rummaging through the dark blue bag. She extracted a bottle and began shaking it as she handed Mary a pacifier. Mary took the pacifier and deftly put it in her mouth – the deftness was a good sign, wasn't it? – and half-heartedly chomped on it. I took the bottle and Nannie leaned forward and removed the pacifier while I eased the bottle into Mary's mouth. It was a routine we'd perfected to forestall the crying.

The trip seemed interminable, but we finally reached downtown Dublin. The driver was weaving in and out of the bus lane on a street of stores and office buildings. The city centre was alive with people, and the lanes of small cars moved sluggishly; bicyclists darting in and out along the kerb, making better time. The driver gaped through his windscreen at a cyclist who had cut in front of a double decker bus. 'Look at that fellow,' he said, shaking his head and muttering. 'Worse and worse, that's for sure!' He was rocking and bowing against the wheel as we crawled along, touching his hand to his hat in salute to other taxi drivers. At length I saw the row of houses adjacent to the Holles Street Hospital. Posted on one of them, which had a large yellow door and polished fittings, was a brass plaque – shiny, discreet, verging on elegance. 'Neurophysiology Clinic', it said. I would have preferred being anywhere else.

I paid the driver. We walked up the steps, Mary still swathed in blankets, Nannie with her navy carryall trailing along, everlastingly tucking at Mary's loose ends. I shifted the child in my arms, opened the door and stepped in, Nannie following. My heart was thumping in my ears, beating so fast that I felt certain the receptionist at the wooden desk would hear the pounding. My throat was tight. My voice, when it came, seemed far away. The girl smiled, motioning to a row of chairs. Nannie and I walked over and stiffly sat down. 'Lovely day,' the receptionist said to Mary. The child stared up, her head falling forward then jerking up as she tried to keep the receptionist in her line of vision.

What kind of examination would Mary be given at a neurophysiology clinic? Would it hurt her? Would there be needles? Mechanical devices? Wires? X-rays? My ears were burning now. I imagined Mary being strapped on to Frankensteinian machines and plugged into electric shock circuits.

I heard the girl call my name. She rose and walked to a moulded door and pushed it open for us to enter. Inside was a substantial room, with a red-patterned carpet on the floor and a large desk. The wall, covered with all manner of documents and degrees, suggested a lawyer's rather than a doctor's office. We sat in chairs in front of the big desk, facing tall curtained windows. It was a lot like a judge's chambers.

'Good afternoon,' came a voice, from behind us, as though from a long way off. It was Dr O'Brien. In quick strides he reached his desk, his eyes searching its surface for the appropriate folder. Without looking at us, he found and opened it and read aloud: 'Mary. Mary Collins. Yes. She was born in June, and was with us for, let's see, seven weeks.' He continued to read silently, then lifted his head and condescended to look at us.

'Mrs Collins, when did you first notice that Mary seemed to have problems?'

'I didn't,' I said. 'I mean, we all knew she was premature, you see. And we thought she was taking a little longer to catch up.'

Dr O'Brien sat back, his face expressionless. 'You were not aware that at this point the baby should have developed further than she has?'

Was this an indictment? I rushed the words.

'Well, I was aware that she couldn't roll over yet. And couldn't sit up, of course. But I thought that all she needed was more time.' I summoned my expert witness. 'Dr Webb told us that, since she was nearly three months premature, we should deduct three months from her age – we weren't to expect her to do things on a normal schedule.' I cleared my throat. 'We weren't to expect her to develop according to the book.'

'I see.' He rifled through the folder again. Getting up, he said, 'I'm going to examine Mary. Take off her outer clothing, please.'

I shook Mary free from the blankets tangled about her, and removed her jacket. She began to whimper and Nannie tried to soothe her. 'Good girl, Mary. That's a good girl.' I handed her over to the doctor, who held her out in front of him.

'She's very stiff indeed,' he said. To test her reflexes he pretended to let go of her. As Mary felt herself drop, she tightened up, her fists curling into little balls, her legs thrusting straight down, and began to scream, with room-filling piercing cries.

'Remove the rest of her clothing now,' he said, handing Mary back to me. She continued screaming. When I came to her little shirt and her diaper, he signalled me to stop, and took her again. He examined her body, then began trying to get her attention. She ignored him. Finally he took a set of keys from his pocket and swung them in front of her. At first she paid no attention, her face screwed up, her eyes shut tight with her screaming. He shook and jangled the keys, passed them to a spot above her head, shook them again. Her head turned towards the sound. He passed the keys to the other side. She turned her head again, opening her eyes, straining to see.

'Nothing wrong with her hearing,' he said, putting his keys away. He began to flex Mary's legs and arms. He struck each knee in turn with the side of his hand. She continued to lie there, her mouth open, screaming.

'Can she crawl?' he asked.

'No,' I said, looking at Nannie, who shook her head. He had Mary on the floor now, on her stomach. He dangled the keys in front of her. Still crying, Mary paid no attention to them. 'She rolls,' I said. 'I mean, she can't turn over but she rolls on the bed. It gets so cold in the house, we can't put her on the floor. She hasn't had much *chance* to crawl. We've been very careful to prevent her catching cold, since she was so premature and all – '

He knelt down before her and took her head in his hands, turning it slowly from side to side, watching her arms and legs. As he turned her head to the right, her left limbs moved together. When he turned her head to the left, there was a reflex crawling movement.

He brought her back to the table.

'You may dress her,' he said. When her clothes were on her again, I held her on my lap and patted her. But she continued to cry.

Dr O'Brien made some notes and closed his folder. He looked at Mary and she quieted a little. 'She's suffered brain damage,' he said. 'Her left side is more affected than her right side. I think, however, that it is too soon to make any prognosis.'

This was it, then. Now there could be no pretending. This was the definitive word. I had a right then, to feel sick at heart. I stared at Dr O'Brien.

'Did you understand me, Mrs Collins? I said Mary is brain damaged.' He was insisting, his tone very distant.

'Is that cerebral palsy?' I asked. 'Are cerebral palsy and brain damage the same thing?'

'Cerebral palsy is a more general term – meaning any kind of insult to the brain which results in an impairment of motor ability. Brain damage is more specific.'

'I see,' I said, meaning I didn't see at all. They still seemed the same thing to me. Or 'damage' the insult, 'palsy' the condition. For his own reasons Dr O'Brien preferred to say 'brain damage'.

'More specifically, Mary has spastic diplegia.' He was writing in the folder as though inspired. 'Both sides, and both upper and lower limbs are affected.'

The words 'spastic diplegia' were barbed words. Spiky and sharp. Ugly little black, flinty, charged, wire-like words. I dared not get too near them.

'Brain damage.' I retreated to that ugly enough term, repeating it, madly bent on compromise. The words were far less objectionable than those newer words.

'You're sure?' I said.

He looked surprised. 'Of course, I'm sure. These things happen, you know. Mary had a great deal of respiratory distress. At birth she weighed less than three and a half pounds. Much too young to be born – '

'But she did so well,' I insisted.

He wrote something on a slip of paper. 'Yes, she did. And I hope she will continue to do well.' He put his pen down and stood up, coming over to me with the slip of paper. Nannie reached for Mary and began to put her jacket back on. He handed me the slip of paper. On it was the name of Dr Ciaran Barry, director of the Central Remedial Clinic in Clontarf. Dr Webb had given me that same name.

As soon as we returned to the house I went to Mary's room.

'I'm going to take her upstairs with me for a while, Nannie.' I said, lifting the little child up to my shoulder. I felt I hadn't spent enough time with her, played with her and talked to her enough.

'She was up very early this morning,' Nannie warned with a sniff. She smoothed the bed covers and straightened the pillows. She began folding some clean clothes on the end of the bed.

I brought Mary up to my own room, next to the sitting-room. It was warm in there and quiet. I could hear Marlene, the wall between the rooms muffling the rat-a-tat-tat of the typewriter. I closed the door. Holding Mary, I walked back and forth across the room, talking to her.

'Why, Mary? Why?' I reproached her.

I could feel her small warm head nestled in the crook of my neck and against my shoulder. Her hair, still baby fuzz, held her body heat, and she seemed frail – of no substance, only a warmth and lightness, fluff and feathers and a beating heart. I held her tight and hugged her, patting her back. She grimaced, her head thrusting away as she tried to look at my face. She gave me an open-mouthed grin, then collapsed again, resting her head against me, the fingers of her right hand stiffly clutching my jacket.

Still like a tiny bird, I thought, remembering when I'd first held Mary, and how her fragility, her china-doll-like tininess, had shocked me then. The nurse had led me to the little room where the warming cots were. By this time Mary had graduated from an incubator to one of those enclosed and sterilised plastic boxes whose temperature was kept constant. She was so very small and thin, almost all bone, her ribs showing beneath a delicate layer of skin. She was being fed by a stomach tube and was gaining weight, they said. Her increase must have come in her length because she had no fat on those twig like bones.

I sat down on the chair opposite the box, thinking I'd only be allowed to watch Mary and study her awhile – perhaps reach in and touch her; my hands were scrubbed and I was wearing a sterile gown. Then, astonishingly, the nurse took Mary's tininess from the plastic case. The nurse was gentle but the little thing seemed startled; her limbs stretched like the petals of a flower suddenly unfolding.

Then the nurse thrust her towards me.

'Now?' I said, aghast at the idea of handling her.

'She's a grand girl,' the nurse said, in what struck me as an extremely loud voice.

'Oh, no! I don't think I could hold her yet.'

'Why not?' The nurse was not at all tentative.

I drew a deep breath and cupped my hands together, palms upwards, as she placed Mary firmly in my keeping. Her eyes open, her tiny head fitted in the palm of one of my hands and her little bottom into the palm of the other. A small, plastic-covered paper diaper bunched itself awkwardly around her. Her limbs waved more slowly than they had in the first startled reflex. Nothing jerky about these movements; instead she was like a dancer executing a graduated series of steps, like a swimmer in an underwater ballet. She had a long thin face with visible cheek bones, a pipe of a neck; her incredibly long tapering fingers, no thicker than straws, curved and curled as she rested in my hands. She stretched, her legs flexing in slow thrusts and her long straight toes fanning out. She was so solemn, so quiet; so very, very tiny. With her visible skeleton, with her elbows and wrists and knees so prominent, with her long thin delicate feet, she didn't look like a baby at all. The nails on her fingers and toes looked like tapioca pearls. Her head – warm tiny head resting in my right hand, so very lightweight, and no larger than an apple – was covered with a downy softness. It was not so much a head as a little skull, its alizarin crimson tints of skin edged with shadows of cobalt.

Mary's head was still, the rest of her waving and moving restlessly. I was afraid to hold her tight. She was too tiny for me to hold in my arms. So I kept her head in my right palm and with my left hand I covered her with the white blanket and tried to edge her against my stomach, tried to pat and nudge her and make her feel secure against me, still holding her head in my palm, while I tried to talk to her.

'Mary,' I whispered. 'Mary.' She didn't respond. As I

pressed her softly against my lap, she quieted down a little and blinked her eyes, her fingers stroking the air.

'So Mary,' I kept on, speaking louder this time, like the nurse, 'here we are.' I felt awed. Formal. Should I continue? *Allow me to introduce myself, Mary. I'm your mother. I welcome you here and I hope you enjoy your stay. I'm speaking on behalf of your father and your sister and your brother. It was so good of you to decide to stay with us and not go away . . .*

In the hospital soon after Mary's birth, the mother of another child had given me a relic of the stigmatic Padre Pio, and a pamphlet about his life containing prayers asking his intercession for special favours. The woman, one side of whose face was marked in mottled deep red, spoke with a slow cultivated voice. 'Pray to him,' she said, carefully enunciating. 'I have so much confidence in him!' Too magical and simple, I thought. But what had I to lose? I'd taken the card with its attached relic. Each of the five days I was in the hospital after Mary's birth, I'd dutifully read the prayers, pleading for her survival. I'd even given the card to a nurse, to place in Mary's incubator.

'And just look at you now,' I said to Mary as I put her on the bed, trying to sound cheerful. 'So round, so dimpled – '

But my heart was heavy as I studied her lying there, trying to thrust her head back, her right arm moving but the left one nearly inert. She began to cry.

Just then there was a tapping on the door. Not Marlene. It was too soft.

'Come in,' I said.

The door opened and Nannie stood there, nippled bottle in hand. 'She has to come now. She has to have her juice.'

With soothing clucks Nannie carefully picked Mary up and took her back downstairs.

The next afternoon a woman who had been doing some typing for us brought me some medical textbooks she'd found on the shelves of her rented house. 'It'll give you an idea of the problem,' she'd said. 'It's worse when you don't know what to expect.' I thanked her and took the books to the desk, a thousand questions on my mind. The books smelled of old glue and dust, and were full of abstract language and technical diagrams and contained photographs of human anomalies. How little I'd known about human deformity!

Of course I'd seen such pictures before. And as a teenager I'd been an aide in a children's hospital ward. When we'd lived in Peru, before I went to college, I'd even taught in a leper colony. I thought I knew all there was to know about human suffering, about physical debilities. But none of it had ever touched me. I'd assumed that such things would never happen to me or to anyone I loved – certainly not to a child of mine. According to the fine print in one book, twenty-five per cent of those afflicted with cerebral palsy were severely retarded, fifty per cent were mildly retarded and only the remaining twenty-five per cent would have normal intelligence. Bad odds, I thought. *Her face has no worry lines*, I remembered Dr Webb saying. I decided then that it would be less painful if I simply accepted it as fact that Mary would be among the seventy-five per cent who were retarded. But how seriously retarded would she be? Would she be able to improve? Would modern medicine and therapy find a way to cure her?

I was shocked when I came across something that flatly denied any such hopes.

Brain damage, one of the books said, was irreversible.

A week later I went to see Dr Barry at the Central Remedial Clinic. He would be the man, I hoped, to dispute the other doctors' findings. Dr Barry was blue-eyed and dark-haired; his manner was cordial. He took his seat at the large modern desk in the spacious office and poised his pen over the sheets in front of him. Mary was on my lap, and Nannie in a chair next to me.

'Do you have any other children, Mrs Collins?' Dr Barry asked.

'Yes,' I answered. 'Two.'

'Then Mary is not your first child,' he said, looking up brightly.

'No,' I answered.

'Then you're fortunate.'

How could he say that? How could I even think in terms of being fortunate in Bonnie and Mark when Mary had suffered these hideous enchantments? I knew what he meant, yet it seemed a crass thing to say. As long as it wasn't the first one, Mrs Collins. Two out of three, Mrs Collins – That's not so bad!

He stood up and took Mary from me. She began to wail. He walked about the room with her, talking to her and feeling her legs. He conducted the same tests as Dr O'Brien had. I stood next to her, stroking her head and holding her small hand. She had become entirely rigid again. Her legs, stiff in front of her, jerked upwards as she screeched.

'Can you roll over, Mary?' he asked, finally, taking her hand from me and crossing it over her chest. He pulled her towards him.

'No, not really,' I said.

'Yes, she can!' Nannie interrupted. 'When she's had a good sleep, she can roll over on the bed.' Nannie put her hand on the examining table, giving its brown surface a disdainful pat.

'Oh,' he said, flashing a broad smile at Nannie. 'Good. Good! And how about this – does it get caught?' He pointed at Mary's left arm, pinioned under her.

'Yes,' Nannie and I said in unison.

He laid Mary flat on her back again and extended both

51

her arms above her head. 'Then you'll want to do this with her,' he said. 'The arm that usually gets caught, hold it up above her, do you see?' He extended Mary's left hand above her head; he took her right hand and drew it towards him. Still crying, Mary slowly turned over, seeming almost to do it by herself, her arm no longer hindering her. Surprised to be on her stomach so quickly, she stopped crying and opened her eyes, her head bobbing as she looked around, her face all red and wet, her nose runny.

'Good girl! Good girl!' said Nannie. But it was the voice she reserved for occasions when she felt a child was being urged beyond all endurance.

Then the room was quiet. Dr Barry was busy writing.

'Will she ever walk?' I asked him.

He looked bemused. 'Perhaps. She may.' He resumed his writing. Finally, putting his pen down, he began slipping pages into various folders.

'And what about her mental ability? Can you tell us anything?'

'Oh, no!' He shook his head emphatically.

'Why not?'

'We never test a child before the age of three. In America they may, but here we don't feel early tests are at all reliable.'

'But what about school?'

'Mary will go to school,' he said reassuringly. He sounded like Tom.

'And after that?' I demanded. I visualised silent grey hospital corridors, crippled figures in wheelchairs –

'Why are you worrying about the future?' he asked, smiling again. 'Your daughter is still so young.'

'Yes, I know.' But that's the way I think, I wanted to say. If in the future I could see some comfort and promise for Mary, the present would be workable in terms of that.

But if what lay ahead was a downhill road, with this pretty little girl destined to slide off into a vegetable or animal existence –

'For the present she'll come to the clinic three times a week. She'll receive therapy, but you'll be observing, and the therapist will show you how you can continue the therapy at home.'

He sat on the edge of his desk now, his arms folded on his chest.

'What about the cost?' I asked.

He looked surprised, 'In Ireland all physically and mentally handicapped people are taken care of by a government fund.'

'Oh,' I said, in an awed voice.

'At the clinic you will of course fill out various forms. When these are processed Mary will receive a little green book. This entitles her to assistance of various kinds. Special therapy, braces if she requires them. Drugs. Even a wheelchair. Whatever she needs.'

'A little green book,' I repeated. Coming from America as I did, I had to feel a surge of gratitude. This was a civilised country! Was their humaneness, at root, a compassion born out of the centuries of tragedy? Or was it simply their gregariousness? I had often sensed in the Irish an underlying current of wild interest in others' activities. They were always expectant, weren't they, when it came to human interaction? – as though wherever two or three were gathered together, something unanticipated but satisfying or important or even electric might occur. And their culture fed the flame: their conspiratorial get-togethers, their intimate entertainments, their carefully managed eccentricities, their humour like quicksilver.

But my heart was pounding again.

'Is there anything else?' Dr Barry asked, tilting his head to the side in a way that encouraged conversation.

'No. I think everything is clear.' I was lying. I had so many questions about the future. But I couldn't articulate them. I looked over at Nannie. She sat there, impassive.

'Well, then,' the doctor said cheerfully. 'Let's see what we can do for Mary.'

He walked with us to the door, and opened it, directing us to the physiotherapy department down the hall.

Mary was clutching the neck of my sweater. 'Thank you! Thank you very much!' I was ashamed to be so effusive.

The doctor smiled and closed the door.

We walked out into the main hallway, a broad polished corridor, towards the physiotherapy office. From there we were sent on to the gym, to see the therapist, a Mrs Fenton.

'I think this is the room,' Nannie said. She stood in an open doorway, hesitant. She coughed, assuming her solemn look; she was a nurse, a professional. We walked into the room. It was vast, with big mirrors on the walls, and mats everywhere; in it were toys, platforms, large wedge foam constructions, huge plastic balls. There was a variety of gymnastics equipment – ropes dangling from the ceiling, jungle gyms, rings, trapeze bars, ladders.

A young woman was sitting with an older boy on a nearby mat.

'Mrs Fenton?' I ventured.

The young woman rose and came over to us, honey-coloured hair framing a smiling face.

'Dr Barry has just seen my daughter. The people in the office gave me this for you.'

She took the slip of paper and went over to her appointment book.

'Mary, is it?' she asked.

'Yes.'

'Good! Three times a week, then. Would you prefer mornings, or afternoons?'

'Mornings, I think.'

'How about eleven o'clock?'

'Eleven will be fine,' I said, my voice falsely cheerful. I shuddered, thinking of all the work I had to do.

Beside me Nannie was watching children in the room being exercised. 'Tsk, tsk, tsk,' she said, as she did whenever she disapproved of something. It was a kind of tic she had; someone else might tap a foot or pull at an earlobe. She was never aware of this; it just twitched out of her.

Mrs Fenton came over to look at Mary, bending to face her.

'Mary!' she said, in a musical and vigorous voice. Mary's lip quivered. Mrs Fenton patted her pink arm. 'Now, now. We'll become friends, won't we!' She smiled at Nannie and me and then, as she turned to go back to the little boy, called out to us.

'I'll see you next Monday then. All right?'

'Tsk, tsk, tsk,' went Nannie, as I nodded and waved good-bye.

Grotesques

As we walked through the main hallway, I saw a red-haired couple sitting at the far end of a row of chairs. With them was a small red-haired boy of three sitting back limply in a sling stroller parked between his father's legs. I kept glancing at them out of the corner of my eye. Something about them startled me at first, I didn't know what. Then I realised that it was the way they were slumped there, the woman's mouth hanging open, the man staring ahead. The child's face resembled the parents', the mother's particularly, except that it had a vacant look.

'I'll bet they've just found out!' I said to Nannie.

'Who? What?'

'Those red-haired people. I'll bet they've just been told that their little fellow isn't normal.'

Nannie, absorbed in thoughts of her own, only frowned.

'Just look at their faces, Nannie,' I persisted. 'You can see it written in their eyes. Poor things.'

We were walking to the lobby desk.

'What do you think, Nannie?'

'I don't know,' she said. 'It's too much. Mary's too young. All that exercising and everything – '

'But they want to start early.'

'Too early.' Nannie glared, not at me, but at the desk where a young man on crutches stood answering a phone. I gathered he was in charge of the switchboard. Nannie looked at him as though he were responsible for the entire outrage. 'Tsk, tsk, tsk,' she said.

'If you'll take Mary, Nannie, I'll get him to ring a taxi from the rank.'

'Good Mary,' Nannie said, lifting the child and patting her back. As she walked over to a black vinyl chair near the doorway, I could still hear her 'tsk, tsk, tsk.'

We talked little on the way home. Mary was asleep. Her peaked cap kept bobbing up and down like a scolding finger. I could no longer entertain the notion that Dr Webb or Dr O'Brien had leapt to an unwarranted conclusion. I could not pretend any more.

I would remember this day in mid-March as the day the screaming began. It was a piercing sensation, shrill, sharp, and high. It was not really a scream made of sound but the pinched-tight, strangled feeling that comes on the verge of a scream. It was in my centre, in some deep partly physical, partly mental, place. I did not actually let go. It was a screaming without screaming, far down in some subconscious depths where reality has not yet been tamed by words. All the way home I was aware of this screaming, expecting it to overpower me, hoping it would subside.

Walking Mark home from Miss Murray's next afternoon, I saw a stocky little man with a young girl of perhaps fourteen or so, who wore her dark short straight hair in bangs. Her dark eyes blinked wildly, and she seemed in constant danger of falling as she limped along the sea-front at his side. Her arms were swinging and flailing as she moved in tortured jerks alternately from one foot to another, her tongue protruding with her exertions. After the first quick glance, I avoided her, looking instead at the little man. Probably he was her father; he had the same dark hair and eyes and sallow complexion.

Mark yanked on my hand. 'What's the matter with her?' he whispered, pointing his finger at the girl.

'Don't point!' I said, seizing his arm and slapping it to

his side. 'Don't ever, ever point like that! Mark! What's the matter with you?'

Mark looked up. Pouting, he took his hand from mine. He kept glancing furtively at the two people. Under one arm the man held a folded newspaper. There was an air of contentment about him. As they passed us, I could see that the man, who had a very kind face, appeared not to have noticed our flurry of looking and whispering and reacting. I could hear the girl breathing heavily; she was excited and happy. Human life is full of flaws and imperfections and disappointments, I said to myself. You'll get used to it.

When we were home, I tried to explain to Mark why it wasn't polite to stare at people with differences – handicapped people. (I didn't say Mary was handicapped.) Mark listened patiently. Underneath it all he still seemed to think he'd been unfairly treated.

After that I began to notice handicapped children everywhere. Grotesques? I couldn't bear to think of them that way. At bus stops I would see a mongoloid child, a child with leg braces and crutches, a child with a neck brace or a hearing aid. From the window of a bus or taxi I would see children with blemishes covering half their faces, cross-eyed children, children being pushed along the streets in wheelchairs. Where had they all come from? Had they suddenly emerged through some fissure in the earth, at a signal supplied by the doctors? I thought of an illustration in a book of nursery rhymes, showing motley figures in tattered clothes surrounded by children and animals:

Hark, hark, the dogs do bark,
The beggars are coming to town . . .

Panic

Nannie, her eyes all red and puffy, didn't look up when I came into the kitchen one morning.

'I guess Mary will have to go away,' she said loudly.

'What?' I asked. I was startled.

Nannie and I conferred often those days, dredging up scraps of recollection that might relate to cerebral palsy. Many years ago Nannie had cared for a little boy, Harry, afflicted with Downs Syndrome, meaning mongoloidism. When Harry was three, his parents placed him in an institution, the normal thing for a wealthy family to do in that era. Nannie recalled packing Harry's things. She recalled how Harry looked when he was brought to the home. She recalled wondering whether Harry understood.

Nannie had a caved-in look this morning, her hands limp, her hair falling across her forehead. She picked a sterilised nipple out of a kettle.

'Mary – when she's older,' she was saying. 'I suppose she'll have to go away.'

'To an institution?'

'Yes,' she said. 'Like the Kennedy girl.'

Nannie was a close follower of the Kennedy family. She'd clip out articles from newspapers and magazines. She'd rip tidbits from gossip columns and save them. Nannie particularly admired Rose Kennedy. When Nannie talked about the Kennedys it was in a musing sort of way, as though discussing members of her own family or intimate friends. She told me that the retarded daughter, Rosemary, who as she grew older became depressed at not being able to keep up with the other Kennedy children, had been placed in a residential home conducted by nuns, and was happy there.

'It was for the best,' Nannie said.

Later that morning I went downtown to get some technical materials from an art supply store. I was in a taxi, moving past large grey buildings in Blackrock, when the solution to my problems suddenly presented itself. In a kind of vision I imagined a cutaway of one of those grey buildings. I saw urgent figures of devoted nuns gliding across polished brown floors. The nuns passed through sparkling hallways, lined with plaster statues of saints set in niches. A crucifix hung from the wall of each chaste white room. I imagined long refectory tables where crippled children, their wheelchairs and crutches put aside, laughed and played games as the nuns bent over them smiling. I saw Mary in a nun's lap, blankets tucked around her little body in a way Nannie would have admired. The nun hugged Mary, rocking her slowly. At night from the chapel came sounds of Gregorian chant, the plainsong harmonies lulling the children as they were tucked into bed by the happy nuns.

I looked out the window again. On my right was a bright sea. We moved through Donnybrook and then Ballsbridge, past the stylish polygon of the American embassy with its gaudy eagle perched over the doorway.

After I'd bought my supplies, I stopped in at the coffee shop in the Shelbourne Hotel. The counter was filled so I sat at one of the side tables and ordered a sandwich. The room was crowded, so I was not surprised when a heavy-set man, nodding politely, slid into the seat opposite. He picked up the menu and studied it as the waitress brought me my sandwich and coffee. Hearing me speak to her, the man smiled.

'Are you American?' he asked.

'Yes,' I said. 'From New York.'

We chatted idly for a few moments, until his order arrived. The room, filled with people, was very noisy, with the white-hatted chefs roaring at one another, with waitresses calling back and forth beyond the counter, with the clink and clatter of dishes and silverware on the tiled counters and formica tabletops. Amid this discord, there was a civilised sense of contained activity, a certain discretion, above all a consensus as to the limited possibilities of conversation.

'I hope you enjoy your stay here,' the large man finally said, raising his voice above the hubbub.

'I've just learned that our youngest daughter is brain damaged,' I said. I didn't know why I said it – perhaps to deny that we were enjoying our stay. The Irish were too disposed to cheerfulness.

'That *is* a pity,' he said, looking at me sympathetically.

'She's nearly nine months old now. And we didn't know until a few days ago.'

'My wife and I have a daughter like that,' he said. 'She doesn't live with us. She's in a residential home.' I must have looked surprised. 'Yes,' he said, with a wry nod. 'Yes, I know how you feel.'

Told that their little daughter would always be like a tiny baby, never able to do anything for herself, his wife, he said, had been heartbroken. They'd kept the child at home for years, but eventually her care had become more than they could handle.

To me, at that moment, it was more than a startling coincidence – meeting someone else who had a brain-damaged daughter. It was *too* strange. It was rather like some mysterious confirmation that the world I'd lived in – in my mind – had gone, had disappeared. I had evidently left one kind of reality and stepped, as through a door, into another.

'So now she's in a fine place,' he was saying. 'She's well looked after. She doesn't know the difference – '

'With nuns?' I asked quickly. 'Is she cared for by nuns?'

'Yes, she is. And they're very good to her.'

Hearing this I made up my mind that when I returned home I would call all the places for the handicapped in Dublin. I would identify the happy faced gliding nuns who would take over Mary's care. I would visit her regularly, three times a week. No, better than that, I'd go every evening. Mary's nun and I would sit together as the dusk fell, playing with Mary, coaxing her smile, getting her ready for sleep.

The dead weight that had seemed to settle in my stomach shifted and lifted. I felt immeasurably lighter. I was impatient to be back in the house again, settled into the big brown leather couch in the upstairs sitting-room, dialling numbers till I found out where my gliding nuns were.

I shook hands with the man and left the restaurant, weaving my way through the busy aisle, among tense waitresses and the ever-moving crowd.

It was afternoon when I returned. Mary was asleep, as she often was at this time. Racing upstairs to the phone, I settled myself on the couch, took a notebook from my purse and began listing numbers. But my mind was reeling. The screaming began in me again. I would look up a number in the book, go to write it down and lose it. Or I'd get the number all right but lose my place, forgetting the name of the school or institution to be pencilled in alongside.

Finally I was able to begin dialling.

'Hello,' I said to the first voice to answer. 'May I speak to the director of admissions?' That, I thought, will give the listener enough of an idea. But the voice at the other end pressed me for more information. This happened repeatedly. In every instance I would have to explain that I had an infant daughter, not yet a year old, who had brain damage and needed care.

'I see,' the surprised voice would respond. And then: 'Well, I'm sorry. This is not a residential school.' Or: 'Perhaps when the child is older we may be able to discuss her needs, but at the moment you can't possibly place her here.' There would be some irrefutable explanation: 'You see, we only take girls from age fourteen through eighteen.'

'Oh,' I'd say, thanking them. Often idiotically: 'Oh, thank you very much!' After a half dozen calls, I began wildly pressing on: 'Could you please suggest a place I might try?' Twice I was given the name of a St Vincent's convent. St Vincent's began to sound better and better. I began saving up St Vincent's, investing in it. St Vincent's would be the last place I'd call. I would only half hear the successive voices on the phone. When it became clear that there was to be no kind offer to take Mary, I'd refuse to listen further, becoming frantic to finish the conversation so that I could hang up and dial the next number on my list. This, or St Vincent's, would be the place I'd imagined, where the nuns were, where Mary would be loved and cherished.

Finally I made this last call.

'May I speak to the sister in charge, please?' I asked. Not the director of admissions. The Mother Superior. At St Vincent's I'd go to the top.

But it was one of the other nuns. 'Perhaps I can help you. The Superior is not here now.'

No Superior on hand. Well, that was all right. This one, with her nice voice, might be the very nun of my imaginings. It *was* a nice voice! Expectant, courteous, even curious. Was this indeed the nun who walked those sparkling peaceful corridors?

'I want to know if you care for little ones who are

handicapped. I have a brain-damaged daughter and I feel I can't adequately care for her – I mean, I work, you see, and our business is causing us difficulty; I wonder if you could help me; I must find a home for my daughter. Please, do you take such children in? There must be some place where she will be loved and helped.'

'Are you an American?' she asked in a puzzled voice.

'Yes. But we work here. We live here. Everything is very difficult right now.'

'I see.'

'I would like to come to St Vincent's so that you could interview me. I'd like you to meet my daughter. Am I calling the right place? You've been recommended to me. I just don't know enough about what kinds of homes there are here in Ireland.'

'Ah, yes.'

'Places for children like Mary,' I plunged blindly on. 'She will need care.'

'How old is Mary?' She'd repeated Mary's name! I seized on this omen.

'She's almost a year old – in June she'll be a year old.'

'Oh, no. No. I'm sorry. No! That isn't right.'

'Isn't *right*? What do you mean?' I was holding the phone so tightly my hand ached. I felt my knees trembling.

'The baby belongs with the mother.'

The voice was smooth. But it was firm and final. The gliding nun had found me out. She disapproved! Perhaps she'd guessed the truth, perhaps she even knew that I could not accept this Mary – that beneath my worry and fright and panic I was angry that Mary had turned out to be this Mary, and that I could not stomach her, that I wanted the other Mary back.

'We do not believe in separating the baby and the mother.'

'I see.' I didn't see. She'd torn my fantasy from me

branch and root. 'Thank you,' I said. 'Thank you very, very much!' She kept on, trying to be helpful. I heard nothing she said. When she stopped, I repeated my thanks and hung up.

It was dark. What had been daylight was now only a red line on the horizon. Till then I hadn't noticed the sky. I hadn't noticed the room turning chill. Outdoors on the sea road I heard a car whizzing by. Downstairs I heard Mary crying, heard the turn of a tap, heard the older children racing through the hall.

Shame

Tom returned from his brief plunge into Europe the day before the plumber arrived.

I recounted the results of our journeys to the doctors with a kind of bitter triumph. 'But they were so vague, Tom,' I concluded. 'They still don't really know.'

'Pat, do you remember *Down All the Days*?' he asked.

'Yes,' I said, recalling the celebrated book by Christy Brown, a young Irish spastic paraplegic who couldn't talk, and who'd laboriously typed the manuscript the only way he could manage – with the small toe of his left foot.

'Do you recall who treated him – a Dr Collis?'

'Yes. Yes. I remember – the man who designed exercises for him so that he could do things for himself. And who recognised that Christy Brown was bright and could really develop.'

'Well, Dr Collis lives near Dublin.'

'He does?'

'Yes. He's helped a lot of people. If we want to find out what the future holds for Mary, then he's our man,' Tom said. I smiled. Tom seemed very pleased with himself. 'Dr Collis is your only man!' he said, playing on the Irish phrase. 'And he'll be "in the book".' At that time there was a single telephone book for the entire Republic.

I called Dr W. R. F. Collis. His voice was warm and cordial. Would he have time, I asked, to talk to us? I was afraid he would refuse. I spoke too rapidly, almost pleading. I told him of our coming to Ireland from America and about Mary's birth. I said that we'd heard of his work with spastics. Would he see us?

'Certainly!' he said. 'I'd like to meet Mary. I don't know what I can tell you that you don't already know – '

I woke up next morning with an exhilaration I hadn't felt for weeks. Tom had gone off to rent a car for the trip to Wicklow to see Dr Collis.

While he was out, the plumber came to unplug the sewer pipes – their condition the result of one of Mark's experiments. He arrived on a bicycle, his snakes and spade and plungers lashed to the bike's rusty frame. A gaunt fellow in his sixties, with high cheekbones and bushy brows, he wore a jaunty golfer's cap on his head. His trousers were tucked into thick black boots laced with yellow strings; over his white shirt he wore a dark tweed jacket, its pockets bulging and sagging. Big bent bony hands dangled from his loose sleeves, which were patched at the elbows. He began by inspecting the toilets upstairs and down. 'We'll have it all fixed in no time at all,' he announced, leaning heavily on the 'we', as though he were a squadron of plumbers. He slowly made his way to the pipes outdoors. He dug down, separated the cylinders, and cleaned out the clogged mass that had accumulated.

'You'll grow tomatoes here!' he said, as he slung spadefuls of the compacted dark earthy stuff towards dainty little rows of spring parsley and lettuce near the garden wall. 'Lovely tomatoes!'

He cleared and refitted the pipe and repacked the dug-up earth around it. Moving with his spade to the pile near the wall, he began to turn it expertly under the topsoil, lifting the earth and bringing it down atop the dark wet stuff until at last he had it all layered in to his satisfaction. He put down his spade. With his hands, toughened and calloused and grimy, he brushed loose clinging dirt and sewage matter from his knees. His jacket and trousers were covered with all colours of mess and sludge.

His chore finished, he stepped back and grinned.

'Here, now!' he said proudly. 'Look what we've done for you. Just plant your tomatoes there, so!' He marched in to conduct a final inspection of the house, to make certain that there was no remaining blockage and that everything was flushing and flowing. As I followed him in, Tom, his red rented car parked in the street, appeared at the doorway. He nodded, then frowned at the figure brushing past him.

'The plumber,' I said. 'He's nearly done.'

Starting up the stairs, the man put his right hand on the bannister rail, sliding along it as he climbed. 'Do you see that?' Tom said to me, his eyes widening. The fellow continued on up to the third floor, running the water there and flushing the toilet. His left hand on the bannister, he grandly made his descent.

'We're finished,' he said brightly to Tom. 'You're fine now!' He touched his cap to me as he left the house.

'Where's a rag? Something!' Tom was frowning at the rail, making sweeping movements with his hand. Then I laughed, and Tom began to laugh. By the time the man pedalled off, we were laughing so hard we were leaning against one another.

Nannie and Mary were aboard when we set out in the red car for Dr Collis' home in Wicklow. Less than half an hour later we were driving through pastureland near Newtownmountkennedy, and then along a lane leading up a little hill flocked with yellow daffodils to the Collis' house, a low rambling affair. It was cosy indoors, with rugs lying upon rugs, with cloth covered tables and stuffed chairs. The walls were practically papered with photographs and documents attesting to his international eminence in various fields of medicine, from orthopaedics to leprosy. We had heard that Dr Collis had helped Jews

68

flee Holland during the war. With him, when he greeted us, was his Dutch wife, who was far younger than he. Dr Collis, who was seventy-eight, was very soft-spoken and relaxed, with a self-confident manner that somehow conveyed a great sense of self-discipline.

At first Tom did most of the talking, asking questions about how intelligent Mary might be. Nannie and I sat primly in our chairs, taking turns holding the baby, who had plans to fret and cry but was too curious about her surroundings to begin just yet. As Tom voiced his faith in Mary's mental powers, I silently expostulated with Dr Collis, unburdening my shame and all my suspicions: I'd been in labour all one Saturday night while the nurses refused to call the attending doctor away from a dinner party; during the delivery the nurses had turned the baby around by hand; I thought there should have beeen a Caesarian, as had been suggested. Given no chance to ventilate this raucous litany of blame, I began instead to answer his questions, and as I answered them found myself sounding strangely cool and clinical. I'd been carrying her for about twenty-nine weeks, I said; I'd haemmorhaged fifteen days before she was born; the placenta had separated prematurely. I asked whether the condition could have been diagnosed in a routine exam in May. Perhaps, he said, but it was unlikely, that early; bleeding was the usual indication. At that I felt some slight relief from the burden of self-accusation. I asked whether there could have been some slip-up in hospital procedure. Perhaps, he said, his tone calm. Let it alone, he seemed to be saying; it's in the past.

He asked that we take Mary into his examining room. This, with its wood and leather and odd little things, made me think of Dr Freud's study. Dr Collis picked Mary up. She might just as well have been a kewpie doll, her little white body stiff with anxiety, her feet thrust firmly forward, her toes curled under, her arms wedged tightly against her sides, her closed fists defensively crossed over her chest. He began moving her limbs as the other doctors had done, finally dangling her by one of her little legs. When he let her down on to the table she howled inconsolably.

We dressed Mary. When at last we managed to get her to take her bottle, it became possible for us to talk. Dr Collis said that though she was unable to perform certain movements, which meant of course a degree of brain damage, he thought Mary would do well. He kept looking at her; kept referring to her as 'Mary'. I took comfort from his hopefulness, and from his matter of fact and sympathetic manner. How very kind and real he was! But he could not tell me that my little baby was fine, healthy, normal.

We continued talking, and Mary fell asleep. Mrs Collis had fixed an elaborate tea for us. As the pale sun of the late Irish afternoon was pouring in, we gathered around a table in the kitchen-dining-room. Though I felt the Collises' warmth and concern, I was so preoccupied with my inner dissatisfactions that at first I only half heard what they were saying to Tom.

'We've had to hide all the knives and even the scissors,' Mrs Collis was explaining. 'Otherwise he'd try to cut himself up.'

I was shocked when it became clear that they were talking about their own son.

They'd had two boys. The elder had been killed at seventeen in a particularly horrible automobile accident. This younger one, a mute, due home soon from the special school he went to, was in a more or less constant state of rage at his inability to talk to people. When his emotions ran out of control, he'd become violent and try to hurt himself and destroy things.

70

I sat there ashamed. During the entire interview I'd been nursing and even parading my sorrow and disappointment about what had happened to Mary. And they, who had been struck a double blow, who had suffered in each case far more harshly than I, had gone to such great lengths to encourage and console me.

Three quarters of an hour later their son had not yet returned. The sun was setting as we drove off down the daffodil flocked lane, leaving them to their evening and their grief.

Hiding

His two brown cases open on the bed, Tom was packing papers and books on top of sweaters and suits. It was mid-April. He'd been back here again, from New York, for the past two weeks. I helped him put in his remaining books, tucking them along the sides, spines up. He zipped the bags closed.

'Oh, Tom, I wish you could stay – '

'I wish I could, too, Pat.'

'When will you be back to Dublin?'

'Three weeks, I guess. I'll let you know.' He checked his watch. 'I'll say good-bye to Mary.'

We went downstairs, and I followed him, tiptoeing, into the small room. He nodded to Nannie, who was sitting on the bed reading a newspaper, the transistor radio murmuring on the small table. Mary lay next to her, fast asleep. Her little mouth was open. Tom stood next to the bed, looking down at the child, his arms folded in front of him; he seemed lost in thought. Finally he stirred and, whispering a good-bye to Nannie, left the room.

The taxi arrived. I kissed him good-bye.

'Don't worry, Pat,' he said. The smile on his face didn't match the uneasy look in his eyes. 'We'll just do the best we can.'

He was off to New York.

I woke next morning with the screaming inside, muted but insistent. To quell it I forced myself to sit at the desk and go through the pile of paperwork. But the screaming was wilder now, and would not subside. I sat at the trestle table in the bay window, looking out at the houses across the street, with their little low walls enclosing neat patches of dull green. Against the sky, in the distance beyond, lay the line of buildings that marked the harbour town of Dun Laoghaire. Poking above the line were the twin spires of St Michael's Church there. As the bells began to ring the hour, I was swept by an immense loneliness. I stared at the houses opposite, x-raying them, wondering what all the little people indoors were doing, wondering in fact who they were. Some I knew only by sight – to nod to, to wave to, to say 'lovely day' to. Yet I knew the children who lived on the block. They had all come to our house to play. And I knew most of their parents, didn't I? No, I thought, I really knew none of them well. I walked around the room. To my right facing the sea was the big window, deeply recessed and with a sill broad enough to hold the tray containing the liquor and bottles of soda and ginger ale, the shot glasses and Waterford goblets twinkling with rainbows.

That strangling, piercing feeling – if only it would stop! I'd have a drink, I thought. But it was only eleven o'clock in the morning. On the other hand, a drink would cheer me up. I hesitated for a moment, my conscience flaring a warning. Years before I'd learnt that there was always that point or instant of choice; and that, once the threshold of choice was crossed, freedom could be lost forever. Thinking this made me feel even worse. So I dismissed the consideration from my mind, poured whisky into one of the rainbow goblets and drained it. I'd crossed the barrier. At first bitter and sharp, the alcohol became warming, heartening. I poured some more whisky into the glass.

It happened again and again afterwards. I'd take a drink, and maybe another. In a few minutes I'd feel almost lighthearted. And when I'd think of Mary, as I always did, I'd think only benign thoughts. Early one afternoon, when the screaming was particularly penetrating, I decided to go to the pub at the top of the hill. I left the house, hurried up the street, opened the heavy door. It was a family pub, our 'local', and promised not only a gladdening drink but the solace of the smokey darkness. The carpet was red, the windows red and yellow coloured glass. There were round wooden tables in the middle of the room. Apart from a table or two of people it was empty that afternoon. I seated myself on a bench along the wall and ordered an Irish whisky without ice.

Sitting there alone, I knew I was hiding from pain. An older Irish couple came in and sat down at the next table, sharing the same bench. Then came more people, who filled one of the round tables nearby. Greetings were passed; chatter and stories ran quickly among them, above the clinking glasses. Presently the older woman, ordering herself another whisky, sat back. We nodded to one another, and she asked whether I was an American. I said I was. She asked whether I was on holiday.

'Oh, no,' I said. 'We live here.'

'Oh,' she said. 'Well, the mister and I live down in the country. This is our holiday.' Her husband turned to her to corroborate something he was saying. 'Ah, go on!' she said, waving her hand at him. She turned to face me, hunching her shoulders confidentially. She had a birdlike way, and her smile was as quick as the movement of her head. She began to tell me about her son. 'Beautiful boy!' she whispered, her eyebrows lifting. 'Eighteen years old, you know, when he broke his neck in a motor-cycle accident. He's been paralysed ever since. I take care of him all the time, but the nuns are looking after him while the mister and I are away on holiday.' He was staying, she said, in a home for retarded adults. 'He'll be there for a month. I think he likes it – the sisters, you know, and all the religious things.' God! I thought. A year ago I would have felt only disinterested pity. But this afternoon the hurt I felt seemed to receive her hurt, two rivers meeting.

Her son's physical damage was bad enough, she said, her voice a dispassionate whisper, her head cocked to one side. 'But now, his mind's gone off. He keeps thanking me all the time – for taking care of him. And do you know what he keeps saying? He keeps saying I'm like the Blessed Mother!' She sipped her whisky. '*That's* what started it.' She lifted her finger, tapping her head, leaning closer. 'If I'm *her*, then he's *Him*!'

I didn't know what to say to this, so I began telling her about Mary. She nodded and sighed. 'Oh, my dear!' she murmured. 'Oh! Isn't it such heartbreak, having children? But that's the way,' she said, repeating it several times. '*That's the way.*'

Therapy

The station at Clontarf was below street level. With Mary in my arms I climbed a long flight of concrete steps to the road, where a minibus was idling against the kerb, an old man with silver hair in a dark tweed suit waiting beside it.

'You're going to the clinic, are you?' he called out.

I nodded.

'We'll be there straight away,' he smiled. With energetic courtesy, he guided me to the side door of the bus and, gripping my elbow, gave me a good push forward and upward. Holding Mary tight, I teetered on the top step and fell into a seat, squeaking a 'thank you'. He slammed the door and sped around the bus. Springing into his driver's seat, he threw the engine into gear.

'Do you work for the clinic?' I asked as he sped off.

'I volunteer my services,' he said. 'I'm retired. I was a driver for the transit company for twenty-seven years, and I want to keep on doing things. Something for others, you know.' There was measure and drama in the way he drove, sitting straight up in his seat, shaking his head in satisfaction. 'It's a grand place, the clinic is. Wonderful people there!'

We turned a final corner into the driveway of the Central Remedial Clinic, pulling up to the front portico. He raced around to my door. Coming down the steps with Mary, I tried to avoid his grip. But he seized my arm and steered me firmly around the front of the bus, pointing me directly towards the clinic door. His mission fully accomplished, he saluted and went off to his bus.

Recognising the place, Mary began to whimper.

'Oh, dear, not again,' I said. 'Everything is fine, Mary. Fine, fine.' Patting her back, I jogged her up and down in my arms. The young fellow on crutches was on duty at the main desk, fielding phones and enquiries with ease, smiling and joking with the people who passed his station.

'Mary Collins,' I said to him. 'For therapy. Mrs Fenton, I believe.'

'Ah, yes.' As he smiled at Mary, her lip trembled. 'Go to the large exercise room,' he said. 'She'll be with you momentarily.'

In the high-ceilinged exercise room, there were mirrors all around, producing images of Mary and me, images everywhere I looked, moving images which advanced from all directions and from different angles – an infinity of images but each on a separate track, the tracks destined to cross and crisscross without ever meeting.

We reached the corner of the room and I sat down on a bench to wait for the therapist. Two other mothers were there with their children. One of the mothers was very young, and sat on the floor with a little girl beautifully dressed in ruffled pink shift, long white socks and polished black shoes. The child's hair was shiny, with two pink ribbons in it. But she was lying limp on the mat, gazing dumbly around as her mother twirled a ball on the surface in front of her, spinning it like a top; when it stopped the young mother would spin it again. But the child, fingers in her mouth, was paying no attention at all. Another mother sat with a boy, about five years old, who had difficulty using his left leg and would drag it along as he bounced from one toy to another. He half hopped from a round plastic horse and lurched over to a large wheeled toy.

Soon Mrs Fenton came into the room and over to us.

'Mary?' she said. 'Mary Collins?'

Mary's head bobbed up and down as she tried to focus on the slender young woman's face. As she reached out and took Mary from me, she stiffened, screwed up her face and began to shriek.

'Now, now, Mary. Let's see what a big girl you are.' To me she said, above the outcries, 'Maybe we'll have time to talk later.' I shouted a response. 'Yes,' I said. 'Okay.'

Mrs Fenton took off Mary's clothes, leaving on only her shirt and diaper. She held her, still stiff and screeching, toes to the mat, watching carefully for reactions. Then she laid Mary down on the mat and, taking her arms, tried to pull her up to a sitting position. Though Mary was panicky, in a frenzy of anger and fear, Mrs Fenton continued to hold her firmly and gently, calmly trying various positions. Finally she sighed and, getting up, brought Mary over to me. I took Mary and tried to quieten her, bouncing her up and down and patting her back.

'She'll have to get used to me,' Mrs Fenton said. 'She's too upset right now to relax.'

I sang in Mary's ear, and carried her around the room. Still she continued screaming. We went out to the hall and walked up and down. People passing nodded courteously, smiling at Mary. I kept trying to get her to take her pacifier, but nothing seemed to work. Her little face was red and swollen. Finally she stopped long enough, breathing big sobbing breaths, to try to suck on the rubber nipple. I kept trudging up and down the hallway with her till at last she fell asleep. The quiet was a relief. I didn't want to go back into the exercise room. But I couldn't sneak out without her things. So I went back in and, without waking Mary, pulled her clothes around her, put the peaked hat on her head, wrapped her in her blankets, took my purse and tiptoed furtively out to the front hallway. Mrs Fenton was waiting for me.

'She's asleep,' I said, defensively.

Mrs Fenton studied her face. 'She's very tense, isn't she?'

'Oh, yes. She's not used to strangers at all – I suppose

we've been too careful with her. Nannie doesn't take her out much. She's not used to these adventures – '

'She needs all the stimulation she can get. I hope she stops the crying. She will, I know.'

'Yes,' I said, without much conviction.

'Do you notice – she's always trying to thrust her head back?'

'Yes, we thought that was odd. She does it when she's very tired – '

'It's a spastic reflex. You'll want to discourage that. When you hold her, try to sit her on your lap and make her bend forward. And when she's lying down, lay her on her tummy or on her side.'

'On her tummy? She doesn't like it.'

'Well, try to put something around her to keep her on her tummy. It will help her. Or on her side, if it's too hard to get her used to being on her tummy.'

Of course that wouldn't be hard to do. The difficulty would be in convincing Nannie that we must try to accustom Mary to things that gave some initial discomfort. Nannie had become convinced that when Mary thrust her head back she was trying to 'get back to sleep'. Nothing, in Nannie's book, could be permitted to interfere with Mary's sleep.

Other Mothers

On the top shelf above the kitchen table we kept a grocery purse with money for the week's purchases. Marlene or Nannie or I would take it and walk up the hill, dragging the wheeled shopping cart behind us, to a small supermarket, a tidy little place with two checkout aisles. One morning as I was leaving the supermarket with the cart I met a neighbour, Pat Johnston, as she was about to enter. Pat lived up the hill on the other side of the street, and her children often played with Bonnie and Mark. We'd chatted on occasion, but we'd never really had an opportunity to talk at length.

'And how is the baby?' Pat asked, her eyes sparkling with interest. She had a hearty, straightforward way of speaking.

'Oh, Pat,' I said. I didn't know whether to go on, but perhaps Pat would want to know, and would care. 'Mary has brain damage.'

She drew in her breath. 'Oh, I'm *so* sorry. Oh, really I am.'

As we stood on the corner talking, I mentioned that I was going to the clinic later that morning. 'Let me drive you to the station,' she said. 'No point in getting a taxi. I can take you. It's no trouble.'

Mary dozed on the train. This time, however, there was no bus waiting at the kerb above the station. It was a grey day and the air damp. I carried Mary cradled in my arms, a triangular afghan around her other wrappings. A chilling misty rain began to fall, its dull monochrome blurring everything, trees, poles, chimneys, into smudged outlines against the sky. The houses along the street seemed ghostly. Mary lazily opened and closed her eyes as I moved along, undecided whether or not she wanted to be fully awake. I found myself facing the old drumfire of self-accusations, wondering how in the world things had ever managed to come to this pass, how it had happened that I was here in Ireland, of all places, carrying a child of mine to a cerebral palsy clinic in the rain. A year ago, if this had been foretold, I would have laughed. How preposterous! My feet wet, and my hands hurting from the cold? Such a silly story! A wave of self-pity washed over me as I thought of the work piled up on the desk at home, the promises I hadn't kept, the material I hadn't typed out, the phone calls I hadn't made, the overriding hopelessness of things at this point. If only I were free just to dig in there and work my head off. Instead I was here, carrying this little one to the clinic, and facing doing it three times a week. Gnawing at me was the feeling that my life was over, that it would always be this way, that as a penance for what I'd done to Mary I'd be carrying her around forever from clinic to clinic, that I'd never be able to do any real work again for the rest of my life. I was trapped, cornered. The anger welled and overflowed until I felt sick.

My eyes watering, I blinked and looked down at Mary, her small face turned towards me as she slept, dark lashes against her fat cheeks. As drops of rain began to scatter around us, a few fell on her face, fresh as a newly opened flower: her skin translucent and pink-white, little blue veins on her eyelids; the down softening around her hairline and along her cheek. Above the grey drizzly street and below the darkening sky, Mary's face seemed to glow. I flapped a corner of the afghan up to cover her from the rain. Seeing the clinic in the distance, I hurried my steps. When I'd reached the lobby I dropped down on to one of the black vinyl chairs, brushing the rain from the blankets as Mary began to whimper and protest.

'It's all right, Mary,' I said. 'It's all right.'

As the big glass door swung open behind us, a man came in, carrying a girl of six or seven with short dark hair. She was thin and her stem-like legs were cruelly twisted; her arms were bent oddly across her chest. Her head was shaking, her mouth twitching, as she spoke to her father, a stocky man, wearing a tattered wool tweed jacket and poorly made, too short trousers. As he carried her across the lobby towards the hallway leading to the pool, he smiled at her, jouncing her up and down. She laughed with pleasure. Then they disappeared into the hallway.

During her session with Mrs Fenton, Mary was stiff as a hard moulded little plastic doll, but she cried less this time. I stopped with her afterwards at the cafeteria. It was high-ceilinged with lots of open space, light pouring into it from the glass-enclosed interior courtyard. The cafeteria was always open for patients treated at the clinic, parents and staff and at mealtimes it served children who attended the clinic's school. As I walked in I saw at the scattered tables children in wheelchairs, children with crutches near them, children moving awkwardly without props. Mary gazed around, her pacifier bobbing in her mouth, her little body straining as she tried to turn and lift her head and hold it steady. She collapsed and stiffened when her muscles gave way under the strain. Her breathing was deep and absorbed. She steadied herself, seizing my sweater collar, and began building up her leverage again.

I went through the line for coffee. Holding Mary on my right arm, I managed to get milk into the hot liquid. I was carrying it away from the cash register when a smartly dressed blonde woman from a nearby table came up and took the cup from my hand.

'May I help you?' she smiled. 'Can you come over here?'

'Thanks a lot,' I said, sounding, I knew, very American. I followed her to the table, where a small boy sat in a stroller.

'This is Brian,' she said, sliding into the chair next to the stroller. Brian sat solemnly, his body concave in the seat, his arms dangling.

'Hello, Brian,' I said, watching as a smile slowly spread over his face. 'Hello,' he managed to say. All his energy seemed concentrated in his brown eyes, darting from me to Mary and back again. The rest of him remained motionless.

'Her name is Mary,' I said to Brian. I turned to his mother.

'Do you have other children?'

'Five others. Brian's the youngest. He's the favourite, of course; he gets all the attention. We all try, you know, but it's just that no one has the heart to force him to stand so that his muscle tone will improve. He can't do anything, and he won't even try. He seems very happy as he is. And he's always so good. Never a bit of trouble. It's just his motor control, you know. He's as bright as any of them.' Reaching over, she smoothed his hair. He smiled up at her, his head lolling sideways. 'And Mary?' she asked. 'How is she doing?'

'Well, she's the opposite, I guess. Mary's very stiff. We're trying to make her more relaxed. She can't sit up, and doesn't like to lie on her stomach. She's always thrusting her head back, especially when she cries.'

She nodded sympathetically, bending down towards Mary, looking at her closely, stroking her hand. 'Hello, Mary. Mary.'

Mary was frowning, her pacifier still. Then she blinked and looked beyond the woman, the pacifier bobbing again.

There was another woman sitting at the table, bright-eyed and pleasant and fat, holding a girl about three years old on her lap.

'Are you American?' asked the fat woman. Her voice was cheerful. She was shy in a childish kind of way.

'Yes. But we're living here. Sandycove.'

'Such a pretty little girl,' she said, looking at Mary, who patted the table with her right hand, suddenly content. 'How old is she?' Ten months, I said. 'They grow so fast,' she said, circling her arm about her own little girl's waist. 'My little one here, we thought she'd need an operation. But she's going to be fine, with these special shoes.' She squeezed the child, who leaned against her and laughed. Though I smiled, there were in me those little wisps of complaint, of anger even. Other people had children who were healthy, not brain damaged. Anything that was marginally wrong could be remedied by surgery, therapy, diet. Special shoes for this one. Mary continued to pat the table, making soft splatting noises with the flat of her palm. I turned to the first woman. Her name, she said, was Kathleen Sorensen. She asked me how often I had to bring Mary for therapy. I said that I'd just begun coming and was supposed to bring Mary three times a week to a Mrs Fenton.

'Oh, she's very nice,' Kathleen said. 'Brian has the tall red-haired therapist. We're from Cork. We come up only every few months. It's here that he gets his real check-up. I come with him and stay with my sister.

'I'm supposed to work with him at home, you know. We come here to see how I'm doing. But I'm afraid they're dissatisfied with me. They think I don't make Brian try hard enough. They think I'm too soft on him.' She laughed apologetically. 'Oh, I do give in to him. I start feeling sorry for him. He gets so tired standing up. He knows I'm feeling sorry for him, and he gives me such sad looks that I haven't the heart. It's terrible. I wish I could be more forceful.'

'Ah, Kathleen, you do your best. You know you do.' This from Bright-eyes.

Kathleen looked at her, gratefully, sheepishly, leaning forward as though granted a blessing. She straightened with a sigh, 'Ah, I know. So there.' She smiled and turned to me. 'And Mary. When – ?'

'It wasn't until a month ago that we discovered she was brain damaged – '

'But before that you thought she was all right? Oh, dear. I know that was hard,' she said.

Knowing she understood, I wanted to tell the other woman to go away so that I could seize Kathleen by the arm and ask my questions. What is it like, having a handicapped child? Does he depend on you entirely? You have to clothe him, feed him, toilet him, and exercise him – what do you think about that? Don't you think it's terrible? I do. Is this any life for your child? Is this any life for you! What do you think? Tell me, please tell me. Please, please.

'And Brian?' I asked.

'Well,' she began, leaning forward again. Kathleen spoke in a low voice. She looked over and satisfied herself that Brian was distracted, by a storyteller at the next table who had captured general attention. 'At first we thought he was all right. I mean, *I* didn't think he had anything wrong with him. My husband's a doctor. He knew, but he didn't tell me. My mother knew. I just kept putting the evidence out of my mind. You know – you don't want to see. You make excuses.' She hunched her shoulders away from Brian, smiling as she hurried on, 'It was – well, I knew and I didn't know. But I just couldn't keep on pretending I didn't know. Little by little I had to admit to myself that Brian just couldn't do anything.' Now she spoke more slowly. 'He was sweet and happy, such a darling baby. But he kept getting bigger and bigger – and still he couldn't even sit up. He was floppy all the time. Then I just knew.'

85

Bright-eyes' little girl was sitting on her lap eating a cookie. The woman seemed interested in what Kathleen was saying, but her smile was too broad, the curve of her frame in the chair too relaxed. She was too gay, too happy, like a child listening to an adult's talk, eager to please but uncomprehending. Now she was pretending to squeal with terror as her child played at putting the cookie into her mother's mouth 'No more!' she exclaimed. Delighted, the child snatched the cookie away from her lips then jabbed it at her again.

'What about the pain?' I asked Kathleen. 'Of *knowing*, I mean? And does the pain ever go away?'

'Of knowing about your child? Yes – well – oh, yes. It's just that you have to go on.'

Thinking she was going to moralise, I felt ashamed I'd been so blunt in asking. But Kathleen, with a glance at Brian, was not going to preach to me. 'I was just horrible about it,' she said with a half-smile. 'I cried and cried. Who would take care of him when his daddy and I would die? I kept worrying about the future! Schools – oh, everything! But I guess I just got used to things. Sometimes I do worry a bit, now. But it's useless! And I'm so busy. In a house with six children there's never a dull moment.'

'Yes, I can imagine,' I said politely. Her time was all taken up with children anyway. She wasn't a working woman. Her husband was a doctor, so there'd be security, and leisure. She couldn't understand, not quite, the distress of trying to manage a handicapped child and at the same time having to work. Kathleen was the first woman I felt I could ask the real questions I couldn't ask the social workers, the doctors, the professionals – but she wouldn't know the answers to my kind of questions.

Yet there was still another big question, wasn't there?

'Sometimes I feel Mary's brain damage was all my own fault.'

I said this lightly, under a kind of compulsion, speaking the unspeakable to a stranger. I was afraid that everyone in the cafeteria would turn around, if they heard, and gape at me; dozens of pairs of eyes staring in embarrassed silence, shocked, accusing, contemptuous. There would be pity, most of all, for Mary. Heads would shake, the murmuring would begin, the whispering to one another –

'When I found out about Brian I kept blaming myself for taking time to put clothes in the dryer!' Kathleen said. 'If only I'd gone directly to the hospital! Instead of running around doing little things – one thing here, one thing there. Afterwards I kept thinking, if only I hadn't done this, or had done that!'

Bright-eyes chimed in. 'Hindsight,' she said.

'Not really!' I said, leaping to Kathleen's defence.

'No,' Kathleen said. 'It's not hindsight. It's just that you always want to feel you're in control. You're not. Some things just happen. There's good luck and bad luck. Afterwards you think about it. You want to say that you *caused* it – the bad luck. But you didn't really.'

'I guess not.' I had to pretend to agree with her. But with me it was different. It wasn't just little things, like putting clothes in the dryer. It was the big things – working, a transatlantic move. And most of all that when I'd first arrived in Dublin I hadn't even gone to a doctor. I felt an awful, sick wrenching. I was getting exhausted by this pretence of normalcy and acceptance. Mary was bored. Her head thrust back against my chest, she made whimpering sounds. Her legs straightening, her arms hardening against her sides, her body stiffened like a papoose on a board. Mary accuses me, I thought, even if they don't.

'We'll be off now, Kathleen,' the fat woman said, standing up and slinging the strap of her pocketbook on to her shoulder. Wrapping her sweatered arms about her little girl, she cheerfully lifted her up. The child laid her head on her mother's shoulder, relaxing against her mother's large breast. As they walked away, the child's chubby legs hung down, swinging heavily from the weight of the clumsy shoes.

Nannie Care

With Marlene's help working against deadlines, I was
finished by early May with the design, layout and paste-up
for two large illustrated books. I didn't have much time to
be with Mary, who was still on no real schedule. Nannie
continued to keep Mary confined in the little room,
pursuing her own purposes – quiet, contentment, sleep.
Whenever I tried to hold her, Mary became restless.
Nannie would appear, tapping a warm bottle against her
arm, and saying, 'She only had a little sleep earlier, she
needs more.' Nannie had taken over the role of mother,
with me in the role of occasional mother's helper.

I hadn't always been exasperated with Nannie. I had
reason to feel great affection for her. She had been the
eldest child in a large Irish family. On the very rare
occasions when she said anything at all about her life or her
childhood, she spoke of her parents with great affection. I
had one image of her – it must have come from some story
she told me – as a serious thin wiry twelve-year-old, riding
off on a bicycle along a twilight country road in Ireland on
some errand for her mother. I had another image of her
sitting with her father while he held her two-year-old sister,
sick with fever, in his lap. The little one had died in her
father's arms. Nannie described how he'd kept sitting
there, holding the small body, crying softly for a long, long
time. I remember watching her face as she told this story.
Sometimes when she spoke about Mary, I would see traces
of the same expression in her mild eyes.

What bothered me most now was that Nannie was
handling Mary as though she were ten weeks rather than

ten months old. Reluctant to take the baby outdoors herself, she became anxious and irritable whenever I proposed a little trip out in the carriage, fussing over the blankets and warning about dampness and chill air. When we travelled together to the clinic, Nannie kept Mary's face covered, protecting her from light as well as air. In the house, she'd walk around with her and talk to her, or hold her on her lap as she sat in the breakfast room and sipped her tea or coffee. Indoors, too, Nannie used the baby carriage as her vehicle of all work, her bulwark and bunker against the evils of indoor drafts and outdoor air. Mary's little crib stood unused. In the carriage, blankets and cloths wadded around her, Mary was protected against movement, activity, light and sunshine. Consequently she had little inclination to stretch her muscles or turn over on her own. Nannie had made the rolling motion of the carriage necessary to Mary's falling asleep; this came to be the lullaby Mary required, and Nannie locked herself into the pattern of sitting on the bed and push-pulling the carriage nearly every time she wanted Mary asleep. Everyone else could see that this arrangement was utterly exhausting Nannie, yet I could not care for Mary in my own way. Nannie still stolidly refused to take any time off. So she wound up with Mary twenty-two hours a day. It was quietly driving me wild. Nannie's way of taking care of Mary flew in the face of all reason and sense. Now it was becoming clear that it violated all canons of good therapy. Give her lots of stimulation, the therapist said; let her touch things; let her play on the floor. 'Put her outside in the carriage to take her nap,' Dr Webb said. 'Or in a playpen. Let the sun shine on her. Let the wind blow around her. Let her roll in the grass and pull at it.' The April air was less damp and chilly. 'You know,' he said, 'it's getting warm now.' He laughed. 'My wife has already been out sunning herself – in her bikini.' I laughed too, thinking of the way the wind blew off the water – I never felt warm. You had to be born here. My own thermostat could never adjust to the weather of Ireland.

'Well, I suppose Mary should be able to take it,' I said. 'After all, she's a native.' I was half joking. Yet surely I thought, some modest ventures outdoors should be possible.

I decided that it would never happen unless she were separated from Nannie. Mary would need another, younger woman to care for her. It would be a loss for Bonnie and Mark, who loved Nannie. Bonnie liked to touch her cheek – 'Nannie has the *softest* face,' she'd often say to me. And she liked to be with Nannie, helping her with Mary and copying Nannie's elaborate and patient ways. Mark would often wake at two in the morning, trotting downstairs to sleep on the bed next to Nannie in Mary's warm little room.

One day I talked to Pat Johnston about my problem. She told me that I might find a girl through a children's home, where she taught cooking and sewing and infant care on a volunteer basis – a place whose charmingly Victorian name was The Cottage Home for Little Children. Pat said she would enquire there, among the staff, and soon afterwards I began receiving calls. To the young girls who phoned, I must have seemed maddeningly indefinite. I was ambivalent: Despite my decision I couldn't imagine anyone taking over from Nannie. And there was the practical question: How would I pay someone a decent wage? So I'd hem and haw on the telephone. I'd call the girl back, I'd say, when I knew just what my plans were, and when the position would be open. Meanwhile would she like to meet Mary? In two cases, the answer was yes. I don't recall much about the first of these visitors – a shy and nervous youngster from a town far away. The second was a warm and cheerful girl of about eighteen who told me she'd had a cousin, named Kitty, who was severely handicapped. Kitty's mother was this girl's 'Aunty Vi' and Aunty Vi had cared for Kitty and stayed with her all the time. 'She never took a holiday at all. Oh, finally she did, but it wasn't until my cousin Kitty was in her twenties and Aunty Vi's mother was dying. Aunty Vi *had* to go then. She was gone for two weeks. Kitty pined away for her. And then, before Aunty Vi came back, Kitty died.'

'Oh, that was *terrible*!' I said.

The girl's face reddened. 'Ah, well, yes. I guess it was. But then there was nothing anyone could do about it – it was all very complicated. And it happened ten years ago –'

'I suppose they all said it was a blessing, Kitty's death –'

'Oh! I don't think so. I don't actually remember. It was just one of those things. Everyone was used to Kitty, everyone accepted her. And then, when she died, everyone just accepted that, too. Oh, of course they *missed* her. But, you see, Kitty was helpless. She couldn't do much of anything. She'd just smile and sit there and talk to herself. Only Aunty Vi could carry on a conversation with her. No one else could understand what she said – her garbled speech, you know. And Kitty only wanted to be with Aunty Vi, really. Oh, she was all right with the rest of the family. She was like a pet. Her brothers would carry her around and try to make her laugh –'

'A pet? She was like a pet?'

The girl nodded and rushed on. 'But it was only when Aunty Vi was with her that Kitty was truly happy. And Aunty loved her – really loved her. It must have been very hard for her.'

'When Kitty died?'

'Yes.'

'Did your Aunty Vi think it was her fault?'

'I don't know. I don't think so. She couldn't help it,

could she? Then, pretty soon after Kitty died, Aunty Vi died, too.'

I sank back into the couch, aghast. Suppose Mary were like that? A *pet*? Would she be? And me? Was I going to be an Aunty Vi? God! Maybe I was. I took a deep breath.

'Thanks so much for coming,' I said, getting up from the couch and hurrying her to the door. 'I'll phone you as soon as I know our plans.'

The End of a Cycle

In mid-May I flew to New York. Instead of Tom coming to Dublin, he had asked me to fly there to work with him for two weeks on pending contracts, one involving a French proposal for a major autobiography. Tom and the publishers were preparing the contract. We had completed arrangements for a book on stress – ironical enough considering the stress we were under ourselves. For myself, I only felt relief from my anxiety when I was drinking. I was really worried. We'd invested in other promising projects, but publishers were now suddenly hesitant because of the economy. It was a tight-money year. There were so many factors over which neither Tom nor I had any control.

I found myself wishing Tom weren't such an optimist. Around him you couldn't even feel sorry for yourself. But I felt ashamed, when it occurred to me that he must feel worse than I, faced as he was with the disappointment of so many of his hopes. One evening we talked for hours about resettling in America.

'Then what you'll do, Pat,' Tom said finally, 'is go back to Dublin and close up the house and office. Our lease ends in mid-June, anyway.'

'And Mary? What can I do about her?' I'd asked the same question over and over. Suppose we brought her here with the older children. We'd have to live in the office where we worked. At eight and five, Bonnie and Mark would present no major problem. But little Mary – with things as they were, and Nannie exhausted now and unable to properly care for her, how could I bring Mary here? A baby, who hardly knew night from day; who needed constant care; who needed therapy several times a week and follow-up exercises at home? From all we'd been able to gather in our sketchy enquiries it was unthinkable that we'd look for a residential home in America – if there even *were* homes providing daily care and therapy for such a child. The only ones we could imagine were either for the indigent poor – frightful institutions staffed by incompetents; or homes affordable only by the very rich. Medical treatment in the United States was terribly expensive. And any good place would have a waiting list a yard long. America seemed hopeless.

I didn't know what to do. Neither did Tom.

'Maybe I can find nuns to take her for a while,' I said, reverting to my original fantasy.

'That would be good. Just to give us a little time – '

'What if I can't?' I said, remembering my futile phone calls in March.

'You'll find something. Just keep trying. A foster home, temporarily?'

'Foster home?' I stood up impatiently. 'Oh, Tom, that sounds terrible! As though we were incapable of caring for our own child – '

'I don't see how you could bring her here. The other two, yes. But not little Mary.'

Tom, I thought, must be dreaming – imagining some loving smiling mother leaning out with open arms to take Mary up and care for her. I sighed. That was his fantasy. The gliding nuns were mine.

'I don't know, Tom. I'll try.'

The next evening I left again for Dublin. It was the end of a cycle in our lives.

Despair and Hope

Back in Sandycove, the pattern was the same – the older children bouncing out to meet me, Marlene fixing her coffee. I rocked Mary back and forth in my lap, studying her face and feeling her rigidness. She blinked at me, her smile wide and happy, pumping her right hand up and down. Her little room was her world. After a journey to the clinic or the store, or any few minutes outdoors, she seemed to find a haven here.

In Mary's bedroom Nannie and I talked solemnly together while she folded clothes. I told her what we thought we had to do, and she shook her head helplessly. Though I was appalled at what Tom and I had planned, my resolve was firm, because every time I thought of bringing Mary to New York, the screaming would wind on, gathering force and volume till I'd remind myself that *somehow* I had to find a temporary home for Mary.

'Nannie,' I began, 'we're going to leave Mary in Ireland for a little while, while we all go back to New York. It's the only practical thing we can do. Somehow I'll find someone to care for Mary till we return. That way she can keep on going to the clinic – '

'And you'll bring Bonnie and Mark to New York with the Mister?'

'You'll come, too, Nannie.'

Wordlessly she placed the neatly piled clothes in the drawer.

'She needs special care, Nannie. It's too much to ask of you, isn't it?'

She gave a deep sigh and sank on to the bed. She seemed

awkward sitting there leaning against the wall, looking at her hands resting limp in her lap.

But I could see that, somehow, during that brief exchange, she had capitulated.

I never thought I'd find much chance to wear my black cape. It wasn't appropriate for everyday use. It was a plain enough cape – just black wool with two slits to stick one's hands through – but it was full length. Because the cape was warm, and because of the dampness and chill in the air, I came to make a habit of wearing it for walks up and down along the seafront at night. I walked the seafront often during those days, my superstition being, I guess, that the walking would somehow transfer its energy to my problems. As I paced I planned what I'd do the following day, who I'd call, what letters I'd write, how I'd sell the furniture, what we'd pack to take to New York with us, what few things we'd ship back, what to do about the overdraft at the local bank, who I could talk to about little Mary.

I took great pleasure, those painful spring nights, in playing a tragic role. I'd lift the black cape from its hallway hook, wrap it around me, and stalk off into the darkness, down to the sea road near the house. I'd go back and forth, back and forth, the folds of the black cape sweeping against my legs. Often, when the sky finally darkened, and when the noise of the wind on the lapping water or the crashing of waves made it impossible for anyone to hear me, I'd scream out curses, yelling and shrieking in what I thought must surely be a terrifying, bloodcurdling voice, shaking my fist at the darkness above: real curses, directed at God. 'How could you do this to me?' I'd shout. 'How could you?' Or I'd scream 'No, no, no! No!,' mounting a blistering campaign of accusation, recrimination and refusal.

Sometimes I would be calm. One night in late May, realising how futile my own tentative investigations had been, I decided I'd go see Dr Webb about a temporary home for Mary. This decision made, I swung around and looked up at our tall house on the corner, looming like a place of gaudy paperboard above its stone wall, illuminated by street lamps and the last glow from the long northern twilight of spring. The softer lights in the windows of the house gave it a cheerful glow, but the walls seemed insubstantial, made of colour, shadow and air, and I thought that if a strong wind blew, the whole thing might come wafting down, the roof tumbling gently into the sea, the walls splitting apart and dissolving after their slow motion fall, wisps of plasterboard blowing like tissue paper into the wind, or like ashes from a dead fire. I walked up the pebbled path, entered the enclosure and, turning the key at eye level, pushed open the door and walked into the hallway whose stairs and bay window were on my left.

Then I closed the heavy door securely against the night.

'I must speak to Dr Webb,' I said to the secretary, and sat down next to a blonde woman paging through a magazine she'd taken from a pile on the round table in the centre of the room. Finished with one magazine, she would pick up another and race through it. The pages made a splatting sound. Sighing heavily from time to time, she swung her right leg furiously up and down. A fifteen-year-old girl was also waiting, and an old fat woman with an old fat man, both dressed in thick woollen suits. Ten minutes each, I guessed. I'd have to wait at least a half hour. So I sat back with one of the magazines discarded by the woman beside me. She went in next, as Dr Webb called her name, smiling and waving her into his office. I put aside the magazine. I couldn't imagine what I'd say to him. Listen, do you know anyone who'd like to have a little handicapped girl on their hands for a while? Any place where a mother can leave her baby while she jets off for a few months? An off-hand question, of minor importance. Is there a safe deposit box where I can leave this child? Nothing really serious, eh? Oh, God! What was I *doing* here? *The child should be with its mother*, the nun had said. Dummy! A mother, and you don't even know that?

It was useless, being here. I could feel the high pitched whine pinching at me. I slumped in the chair. The blonde woman emerged and the girl went in. The old man looked at his watch and nodded to his wife, pulling at his sweater, straightening his jacket. He'd be the next one called. Then it would be my turn, and I'd go in there and talk inanely about something beyond Dr Webb's power to do anything about. He'd only know the places where I'd already been refused. All right, I thought, I'll leave. I'll say to the receptionist that I've changed my mind, say I'll phone him from home. She'll be curious, but she'll mask her puzzlement professionally, she'll smile pleasantly. I'll just open the door and go. I'll walk slowly down the hill towards the seafront, towards our house, thinking of what to say when I phone the doctor. I'll go directly to the sitting-room, ring the number here. And this receptionist will have him phone me back when he's through with the old man there. While I'm waiting I'll have a glass of wine in the semi-darkness of the sitting-room.

The door to Dr Webb's office opened. The girl came out, clutching a prescription in her hand. The old man stood up, beaming, and went to the doctor. His wife joined him, and the three of them disappeared into the doctor's office.

I sat up, tucking in my sweater, brushing my skirt. There was no point in leaving now – no one else here. I could hear chairs scrape in the next room, the old man muffling a cough. I could see the secretary opening and closing file drawers, putting papers away.

There was still that persistent scream. Would it never go away? *Doctor, I have a screaming going on inside me* – NO. Of course I could say that I loved Mary – little Mary with her dimpled hands and fat little fingers and sunny big smile. Then what was I doing, sitting here? I have to leave her somewhere, Doctor, so that I won't have to worry about her. So that I won't have to hear her cry; so that I won't have to feed her and change her; so that I won't have to worry about Nannie, who still refuses to put Mary to sleep on her stomach in her crib, and who insists on keeping her in the house all the time and who boils the bottle nipples then falls asleep till the water boils away and the smell of burning rubber wakes the baby. Nannie and Mary, Doctor, are one another's prisoners, and I can't break the pattern except by a wrenching break, and this means guilty violence; this means criticism from family and friends, who know, as the nun knew, as I know, that the child needs one person to care for her and needs to wrap herself around that one person in love. I believe that, and yet I'm here.

Oh, my God! I cried out silently. Do You know what You have done to me? Why couldn't I be one of those valiant women in the scriptures, patient, faithful, brave against all odds, who put their feet on the road of righteousness, trusting the Lord God to help them? I'm just looking for a way to survive. I'd have been happy just to be on my own, to be able to act, move, work, solve problems; to be free and unencumbered. With a little help from God, yes, but knowing that this was no age of miracles but a colder kind of time, in which God helped those who helped themselves. God (I'd often asked this, storming up and down the strand), where *are* You? I can't even take pleasure in knowing I'm on the right path, because I think what I'm doing is rotten. Yet I honestly don't know what else to do, or I'm not willing to do anything else. Sullen, slumped creature, squeezing your hands on your lap, waiting to ask this unsuspecting doctor where you can leave your handicapped child. You don't want to be bothered – that's it, isn't it? And your vanity's hurt – isn't that it, too? Of your three beautiful children, one has turned out less than perfect. It's true – how terrible! The whirring in me pitched itself higher and I swallowed hard. I didn't even have any pride to keep me warm.

Suddenly the door opened, and the fat old couple tottered out, both of them beaming. Dr Webb followed them, passing the folder to his secretary with one hand and waving to me with the other, as though he'd been choreographed. There was a certain gaiety in his step, probably because I was the final visitor of the afternoon. I took a deep breath and walked across the room, pulling together what shreds of dignity I could.

'And now,' he said, as I seated myself in a wooden armchair in front of his desk, and he in a swivel seat behind it.

'It's about Mary. I need your suggestions, if you have any, as to where I might leave her – ' I saw him sit back a bit, saw his eyes quickening in surprise. ' – here in Ireland, while I go back to New York with the other children.' There I'd said it, spilled out the terrible words, sent them billowing into the room, filling the hollows and crevices, the desk drawers, the wastebasket, spilling out through the keyhole.

'You can't bring her with you?'

'No. I have to work. Things in the business are not – well, we have a lot of commitments to keep, and some problems to straighten out. And I just can't let Nannie keep on caring for Mary. It's too much for her. And we really have no place yet for the whole family to live.'

He listened quietly, tapping his pencil on the desk.

'Could we find a couple who would care for Mary, like foster parents?'

'Well,' he said, sitting up straight and smiling. 'I have an idea. How long do you think you'd have to leave Mary?'

'I don't know. Several months. Until the end of the year, at latest.'

'You know it will be hard on her, don't you?'

'Oh, yes, I do!'

He knew this was a terrible thing. Of course he knew. To leave a child not even a year old with strangers. What would it do to little Mary, who already had so many difficulties? My thoughts were whirring and jamming again.

'The Cottage Home in Dun Laoghaire. It's a kind of orphanage and day care centre. But it's very good. The matron there is very good.'

'The home where Pat Johnston teaches?'

'Then you know it?'

'No. I've never been there.' Its quaint old name notwithstanding, I'd imagined a dark, Dickensian place, with rows and rows of children, in white collars and little grey smocks, eating in a big dining-hall. I'd never thought of it in relation to Mary. 'But Mary is handicapped – she needs so much care and she needs therapy. Do you really think they might be able to take care of her?'

'Ah, they might, they might. I know the place well. I go there, you see, to look after the children. I can't promise, of course – '

'Oh, of course you can't!'

'And do you know that doctors leave their children there while the parents go off on holiday. And the doctors' children love it. They look forward to it.'

'Really?' I was stunned. I'd *never* heard of any home like this. I must have shown my astonishment. He laughed, his blue eyes glistening – pleased, I suppose, that he'd been the bearer of such strange good news. 'It's quite a place. Of course Mary *is* so young. But they'd get her outdoors. They have all the babies out in their carriages in the morning, all lined up. And the girls who care for them – they're all very kind and good. Very gentle with the little ones. It's like a big happy family. The matron there – she's quite extraordinary!'

No nuns. No foster parents. 'Oh, that sounds as though it would *work*!'

'Good. Good,' he said, standing up. 'I'll call The Cottage Home. There's a board there, and before a child is accepted they must review the circumstances. So I'll mention that you'll be calling them. Is that all right?'

'Yes!'

'Oh, and incidentally – '

There was a catch, wasn't there?

'Mrs Johnston's sister is on the board. She's connected with the place – as a social worker. She might even be the one you'd be talking to about arrangements.'

Questions

'How stable is the marriage?'

Pat Johnston's sister came to see me early one afternoon at the end of May. I took her up to the sitting-room. She didn't want to trouble me about personal details, she said. Perhaps I could speak more confidentially with the man she'd arranged for me to see – he was a social worker, too, and he'd be presenting the case to the board, along with his own recommendation.

I was touched by this delicacy. Unnecessary, in a way, because what I had to say I'd already said, to a number of people. But I did think that I might be able to find ways to explain why I felt desperation. It would be a relief to be open with someone who could help.

So it was Pat's sister who drove me, a few days later, to see the man at his office. He was youngish, but patient and tolerant. He listened quietly. I was able to articulate all my confusion – about Nannie, about the children, about little Mary, about the house, about our future. Still I felt uncomfortable. It was not the kind of situation I'd ever imagined myself in – if I'd thought of it at all, I would have imagined being on the other side of this desk, comforting and helping other people, solving problems for parents who had no place else to turn, no one to care for a child. Now I was the one looking for help; in a nightmare reversal of roles, it was I who was on trial. I was 'other people'.

'One thing of concern, of course, is the length of time you'd like to leave Mary at the Home. You do think you will have solved some of these problems by December?'

'I think so,' I said. I didn't know. But six months

without the problem of Mary – her patterns of sleeping and eating, her colic, her outings, her clinic visits, her therapy – it would mean a dark tangled mass being cut away, like surgery without apprehension and without painful consequences. I thought he must surely think me callous, hoping to leave her like this. Six months! In New York I would work. I'd get up early and work late. I'd find time somehow for the two older children; I'd find them a good school; read to them; take them places.

'We plan to come back to Ireland,' I said. 'I don't know how we could get help for Mary in the United States. It's so expensive. You know, the American Medical Association. The greed of the American system – it's a disgrace. We know of no place in America where we could afford to send her for therapy. But we know the Central Remedial Clinic – we know that it's good! We'll solve our problems and come back.'

'Come back to live in Ireland, do you think?'

'Yes. The only problem is income. As long as we have contracts. It's difficult for non-Irish writers and editors to make a go of it in Ireland. We have to do it from our own resources. Certainly I'd have a better idea of how we'll do it after a few months in New York.'

'Yes, I understand.'

I didn't quite see how he could understand. I took out a Kleenex and blew my nose. I was so tense my knees were shaking – it happened whenever I had to speak unprepared before an audience. I felt wound up inside, thousands of strands of possibility hopelessly enmeshed. My mind spun out as a spider spins, swinging down and weaving to catch the reel, sliding down single threads, swinging to get from one to another. They were ingenious, spiders, quiet like the mind. But in me most of it was messy tangle, knotted, hardened, spoiling, rotting, the nauseous constant odour from worrying and fretting, from the decay of thought and yearning. And then I found myself crying. I didn't want to cope with Mary. The social worker knew that. I knew that he knew that. The strands knotted as I sat there, my head down, looking away.

'I just need some time. And I need Mary well taken care of. But not by me.' I crumpled guiltily in my chair. 'I can't right now – I just can't.' I blew my nose noisily, dabbing at the corners of my eyes. What kind of mother was I, anyway? I would never have considered leaving Bonnie or Mark. *But I don't want Mary*, part of me said, wishing she'd somehow vanish. I wanted to turn back the clock, go back in time to where we'd been before – a busy family of four, living in New Jersey, with our main office in Manhattan. Tidy. And now all this instead. Dear God, how could it be this way? Because I chose to do what I'd done. I'd willed the consequences – all this mess, the wages of my wrongdoing. Layers were peeled off, my veneer stripped – down to the original material. I knew I should shoulder my responsibilities – but I couldn't.

Then he asked me about Tom, what kind of person he was. 'How stable is the marriage?' he asked me. At first I didn't know what he meant. No, I said, we're not separated, or estranged. We're not even angry at one another. He asked me about our families, and whether anyone else could care for Mary. No? He asked me about the business, about how Tom spent his time. How much of it did he spend with the family? What was Tom likely to do when we returned to New York? Again, would there be anyone in the family in the United States who could take Mary for a short while? No?

'It will be up to Miss Burrows,' he said finally. 'I do think Mary would be better off with her own family. But under the circumstances, as far as we're concerned, you have more than enough to handle. When Miss Burrows meets Mary she'll have an idea whether she can take her on.'

'You mean she might not be able to?'

'I think she'll be willing. Miss Burrows is a remarkable person. But I'm not a hundred per cent sure. She's the matron. Only she can finally decide.'

'Did you feel he'd try to help you?' Pat Johnston's sister asked. She was driving me home to Sandycove after the interview.

'Oh, yes,' I said. 'He said he'd make the recommendation. It will depend on the matron, though, as you said it would.'

'The only thing they'd really be worried about, you know, is – well, abandonment. That you'd leave Mary there and never come back for her. And now, of course, after meeting you, he'd know there's no question of that.' She smiled apologetically. '*You* wouldn't do anything like that.'

It had occurred to me. Yes, it had, in little split second mental minidramas – what it would be like to leave Mary at the orphanage, go to America and then never come back for her. Family of four jets off to the colonies, disappears, is never heard from again. A comical notion, of course, and I laughed, because it *was* impossible – I *couldn't* do such a thing. Perhaps because I was a coward, enough of a coward to leave Mary there because I couldn't take care of her, and yet also enough of a coward not to leave her there indefinitely – a *respectable* mother didn't abandon her child. Both ways I was a coward.

'No,' I said. 'I just want to leave her here long enough to get things settled and stable again.'

Miss Burrows had a perfect Irish complexion – white fair skin, red cheeks, her hair a glistening black, her eyes navy blue. Originally there had been minor objections to her as matron because of her age – she'd been the youngest ever to hold the position. There were no objections later. Everyone felt she'd done a remarkable job, and she'd been matron of The Cottage Home for ten years now.

'It's like a big happy home,' Dr Webb said. 'It's a bit untidy, but that's a good sign,' Pat Johnston said. 'With her the children come first.'

When Ann Burrows came to our house, I brought her into the little room at the end of the hall. Miss Burrows sat down on the bed where Mary was lying happily, hands and legs moving slowly in the air. Nannie kept arranging and tucking blankets, smoothing the bedcover, plumping up pillows. 'This is Miss Burrows, Mary,' she said in her low soft voice. Mary chewed on her right fist, then smiled as the young woman bent towards her. Nannie sat slumped, hands in her lap, but she'd seemed less tense lately, more willing to accept giving up caring for Mary. Now perhaps we'd found a good place, where Mary could be cared for temporarily. 'I guess it's all right,' Nannie had said quietly. 'If that's what you want.'

At Miss Burrows' request Nannie, using her hands, demonstrated her way of handling Mary, and a carrying technique we'd learned from the therapist. 'Let's see what a big, big girl you are!' Miss Burrows said, as she picked Mary up. Though Mary looked dubious, she didn't cry. I talked about the stiffness and how she thrust her head back, how we tried to massage her feet to keep them limber. I showed Miss Burrows how to sit with Mary and push her forward, flexing her trunk.

'She can't crawl, can she?'

'Not at all,' I said. 'She needs lots of stimulation – '

'Oh, she'd certainly get that!' Miss Burrows laughed.

When we were all having tea together in the breakfast room, I asked her, my heart beating hard, if she thought Mary would be too much for them to handle.

'No. I think not. I think we can manage it.'

'Oh, that's wonderful! But Mary goes to the clinic three times a week for special therapy – '

'Yes, we'll continue all that. I have the car. Someone, probably the nursery mother – there's one "mother" in charge of each nursery – may be able to bring Mary for therapy.' Then she asked, 'When are you leaving?'

'In two weeks.'

'Come over and see us as soon as you can. Later you can begin bringing her things.' We'd bring over the carriage and the crib, I said, and all Mary's toys.

I walked out to the doorway with Miss Burrows. 'Thank you very much for helping us.'

'Well,' she said, her head to one side, 'I hope she'll be happy with us. I'm sure she'd prefer to be with you.'

'Yes,' I said. 'I know.'

But as I walked back to the breakfast room, I felt elation. Oh, yes, if this had to be done, then it was being done under the best possible auspices. This Ann Burrows!

'What did you think, Nannie?'

'She seemed like the kind who would care,' Nannie said, lifting Mary over her arm and returning to the small bedroom.

The Cottage Home

A few days later I visited The Cottage Home. It was the beginning of June.

'It's not a place for handicapped children. And that's better.' Dr Webb had said confidently, pleased with the solution. Yes, I thought, that does make it better. But in the end I was reluctant to go. What if it were a regimented sort of house after all? Or like the places in New York like Letchworth Village – my sister had worked there summers while in college – filled with people who, their individuality lost, wilted and faded and grew stagnant? An impersonal place, run by rule and regulation? As I walked along the street I saw the two-storey red brick and stone building with a brick wall around it. With its grounds, The Cottage Home occupied an entire block. There was the short walkway leading from an iron gate to an enormous wooden door. Within the walled enclosure and to my right, beyond the bushes and trees, was a vegetable garden. I rang the bell, and was admitted by a plump young woman with bright red cheeks.

'Oh, yes, Mrs Collins,' she said. 'Come in, please.'

My first impression was of the scale of the place. There was an entry hallway, opening on to a cool corridor. The high ceilings, the tall doors and lofty windows gave it the feeling of a public building. The dark of the hall above my head gathered into clouds of shadows. There was a row of baby carriages lined up along the corridor near an old battered couch with ill-fitting upholstery. We turned left into a large carpeted room. There were comfortable chairs, couches and reading lamps. There was a massive desk, papers piled on and around it. I stood waiting at a window, looking out at a large lawn. I heard, as though far away, the laughing and shrieking voices of children at play.

The door opened and a sturdy, rather heavy-set young woman with glasses and light brown hair introduced herself. She was Miss Goodge, the assistant matron. Since Miss Burrows was not in, she would show me the Home. She first took me upstairs. At the end of the second floor hallway she threw open a huge door and we stepped into a sunny room. 'It's the Peter Pan nursery,' Miss Goodge said. There were murals on the wall and in the centre a big playpen full of stuffed and inflatable toys. There were half a dozen cot cribs and four basinettes. There were tables and chairs beneath the windows. There was a sink in one corner of the room. The floor, covered with linoleum, was very clean. 'We'll put Mary's crib over there,' she said, showing me a space along one wall. Well! I thought, I *could* imagine Mary in this sunny room. In two of the little basinettes small infants were sound asleep, blankets swaddled tightly around them. I looked at their tiny faces, mouths furiously sucking as they slept. A door burst open and a girl bustled in. She put clean clothes away in a large wardrobe and began whisking about collecting toys. Then, taking a bottle, the girl went over to one of the babies and lifted it gently.

'Time for lunch,' she said, as the child opened sleepy eyes and began to move and yawn. She wrapped it in blankets and marched over to a chair near the window, where she began feeding it.

'The matron's room is next to this one,' Miss Goodge said, as she led me into a hallway, pointing to the door to the room where Miss Burrows slept. 'She listens for the little ones at night.' We walked back into the nursery.

'Do they cry much?'

'Sometimes,' she said. 'But that's to be expected,' she

laughed. I repeated things I'd told Miss Burrows about Mary's quirks – how she didn't sleep much at night, how difficult it was to get her to nap during the day, how she wasn't used to noise or to being in a crib or outdoors in a carriage.

'She'll get used to us,' the assistant matron said. 'They all do. It just takes a little time.'

I looked fondly at the awkward mural of Peter Pan in his garish green suit, a happy smile on his elfin face. I felt anew a grateful astonishment that this place existed.

'When would it be best for me to bring Mary?' I asked.

'Whatever day you'd like. Probably best to bring her in the evening, when you can put her to bed.'

Several nights later I was in the Peter Pan nursery again, but this time I was putting Mary's nightclothes on. I carried her around to get her accustomed to the big strange room. I had my own anxieties to deal with, too, and my twinges and pangs of conscience. I held her tight to my heart, rubbing my cheek against her downy head. She was full of curiosity. But her fingers clutched at my sweater as I settled her into the crib, arranging blankets around her. She began to cry and whimper. Turning her on to her side and rubbing her back, I put a roll of cloth near her cheek, 'for comfort', as Nannie liked to say. There were seven other children in the room, two of them infants, I marvelled that they were all so still, so obediently quiet. Then a small boy in the next cot began moving about noisily. Loosening his covers, he stood up in his crib and leaned over the railing, his finger in his mouth, staring at Mary. She began wailing. After fifteen minutes or so she calmed down. But it was getting late, and I reasoned that as long as I was there it was unlikely she would fall asleep. And the girls would look after her, wouldn't they? I decided to leave. The shadows in the room seemed heavy and critical. In the darkness I resolutely turned away from the crib. I began to move quietly towards the door. Then I heard her begin to cry. She cried out ever louder as I made my way nearer the door. I opened it, stepped into the dark hallway. I closed the door behind me. Mary's crying became fainter as I walked down the hall, down the stairs, to say good-night to Miss Burrows and Miss Goodge as I left The Cottage Home.

A Farewell to Ireland

It was two nights after I'd left Mary at the home. Eleven o'clock, and I was exhausted. A freight forwarder had come to cart off things we badly needed but couldn't carry with us on the plane. I'd worked my way down from the top floor, picking up the odd things left behind – coat hangers, broken toys, newspapers, magazines, dishes, ashtrays, small screws, loose pieces of puzzles, odd mittens and shoes, a half-empty bottle of lotion. I'd been sweeping and wiping the woodwork as I went. I was packing the remaining clothes in the few bags we had. Finally I had to stop.

Marlene had found another job a week earlier and was already working at it. Pat Johnston had invited Nannie and the children to her house for dinner and to sleep overnight. So I was on my own, tying up the last loose ends. Too tired to go any further tonight, I poured myself a drink and went to the bay window seat in the little landing above the front hall. A plastic bucket with cloths and cleanser in it stood at my feet; a broom and dustmop stood against the stair rail. I had the hallway to do, the front room, Mary's room, the breakfast room, the kitchen. I didn't know how I would finish it all now.

This was it, I thought, holding the glass up to the window and nodding to the world outside. I felt the whisky warming me. I nodded to Ireland. I nodded towards Dun Laoghaire, towards The Cottage Home where my little Mary now lived. I felt utterly drained, cleaned out. I thought of my newspaper ad under the boldface heading 'ARTICLES FOR SALE', and all the people who had drifted in and out, poking and probing, snatching at the lamps, at the vacuum cleaner. There'd been the women with curious questions; the women bouncing on the beds to test the springs; the man who bought the filing cabinets and the trestle tables; the elderly couple who had haggled with me over the couch and chairs in the sitting-room, finally taken them for less than a fair price, and yet I hadn't cared. There'd been the breezy wife of a man who had done editorial work for us, who had offered to help sort items and price them for sale and instead had done nothing but sit there, drinking our whisky till she was boozy, then had chosen the things she wanted for herself and loaded them the next day into her small station wagon, driving off with Mark's tricycle tied to the back and our clothes dryer tied to the top. Everything was gone now, except for the two beds. I reminded myself to give the owner's agent around the corner the names of the women who had bought them but wouldn't be able to come for them until a few days after we'd left.

I could hear the waves slapping against the sea wall. I could hear an occasional car running along the road, and could see shadows from its headlights rush across the ceiling. I emptied my glass and collected my broom and mop and pail. I finished all the downstairs cleaning except for the kitchen. Lugging out the debris, I marvelled at how quiet it was outdoors. Afterwards I went from room to room, remembering where the furniture had stood, remembering what had happened during our thirteen-month stay in this house, remembering all the people who had come and gone, and seeing in pieces of carpeting and the hang of curtains phantoms of Tom and the children and Nannie. And I remembered all the various smells of the sea.

It was midnight. I'd hoped to get to the kitchen hours ago, but still hadn't. I stood at the doorway, leaning against the jamb. I just couldn't do it now. In the morning I'd write a note and leave some money to cover the kitchen cleaning, and then we'd have to go. Pat Johnston had offered to drive us to the airport, to get the plane for New York leaving in the early afternoon.

Return to America

'Six months,' I was saying. 'Mary will stay at The Cottage Home six months – until December. Then we'll go back. Or bring her here.' We were in my father's station wagon – the children, Nannie and I – swinging east on to the Long Island Expressway. My stepmother Mary – called Mimi by the children – was driving, my father sitting beside her.

'That's fine,' Mimi said. 'I don't see what else you could have done. How wonderful that there is such a place!'

'Yes,' my father said. 'You feel she's happy there, that she's in good hands?'

'Oh, yes.' My throat was tight.

'I miss her,' said Bonnie. 'It seems funny being here without her.'

'Yes, dear,' Nannie said, patting Bonnie's leg, her head turned away from me, looking out the window, reminding me that in her heart she'd opposed Mary's separation. Nannie wore the grey printed raincoat that looked too big for her, her hair was tucked up into a grey hat with a deep crown and a short turned-down brim, the kind of hat she always wore because, she said, it hid her hair. She moved herself in the seat. Nannie had agreed to come back to New York, agreed to leave Mary in Miss Burrows' hands. Yet though she said nothing directly, Nannie didn't feel I'd done the right thing.

Mark squirmed, restlessly lunging backward and slamming into the backrest, startling Nannie and me on either side of him.

'Sit still, Mark,' I said. 'What's the matter with you?'

In a pout he swung his feet against the seat support. Nannie patted his leg with her other hand. 'Poor Mary,' Mark said. 'She won't have us for her birthday.' Saturday would be June 24, when Mary would be one year old. Nannie sniffed and kept looking out the window.

'There are eight little ones in the nursery Mary's in,' I said loudly. Mimi nodded vigorously, and my father half-turned in the front seat so that he could look at me. 'And besides Miss Burrows,' I said, 'there's a nursery mother, and then the young aides. And so, besides all the helpers, there are two motherly women. I mean, two people who truly care about Mary. She'll have her basic relationships with them.' My voice, trailing away, sounded mechanical. 'They're very good there. They really are.'

Nannie sighed loudly.

'They'll continue bringing her to the clinic,' I said. 'Three times a week, just as we did.'

'Oh, that's marvellous!' Mimi said. Before her first marriage she had been a physical therapist. 'Then Mary will continue with the same people there, won't she?'

'Yes.'

'That's good, dear! I mean, since she's so little it's important that she keep on with the therapy until you and Tom get things straightened out.'

It was beginning to get dark now, a June evening on Long Island, but our body clocks were still on Irish time, and in Ireland it was long after midnight. I hoped that as soon as we reached my father's house the children would go to sleep. And Nannie too. I wanted them all tucked in, safe and quiet. When we woke in the morning little Mary would be having her afternoon nap in her carriage in the garden of The Cottage Home. At noon New York time she'd be having her supper.

'Can she sit up?' my father asked suddenly.

'Not yet,' I answered. 'But she's learning.'

'I see,' he said, looking off into the oncoming traffic, pensively thumping the back of the seat with his hand.

After a two-hour drive we arrived at their home, a little two-bedroom house which sat beneath the shadows of tall maple trees on a side street in Westhampton Beach. The large front window glowed with light. Across the road at the corner was a dark wood, lush with growth that warm summer night. A shushing and murmuring wind rustled the leaves of the trees; the smell was of greenery and moist earth. I had forgotten how tall the trees were – so different from Ireland – tall and black against an indigo sky powdered with stars. Indoors the house was warm and cheerful. Mimi had filled it with growing things. A huge green split-leaf plant towered in the corner of the living-room.

I put the children to bed after dinner, despite their warnings that it was too early for them. I kissed them good-night, and within half an hour both were fast asleep. I sat at the dining-table talking to Mimi and my father. Nannie, a newspaper in her hand, sat half listening and half dozing in an adjoining chair. Tomorrow, I thought, she would go into New York and return to the woman's residence to the little room she'd kept there for twenty-five years. But what would she do now?

Three thousand miles away Mary was asleep in her crib. When she woke in the morning crying, what would they do to calm her? And what would Tom and I do? Everything seemed so utterly hopeless. No new contracts, no new money, and yet our obligations continued.

Next day the air was clear and bright, the sun glistening off leaves whose summery greenness seemed overwhelming. My sister Aileen, always vivacious with her quick wit and ready laugh, came to visit, inviting the children to go swimming at a beach club. As we drove the short distance to the club, I was enchanted by the bright colours of the

Long Island summer, the blue sky, the gleaming white clouds. At the club there were yellow and orange umbrellas, tanned bodies in bathing suits of blue and pink and lime green, bright beach balls bobbing in the sparkling aqua of the pool. After our swim the children and I returned with my sister to her little summer house, a half block distant from my father's. I was struck by the brilliance of everything, by the absolute red of the geraniums in rows beneath the glistening windows with their jutting yellow awnings.

'It's so pretty here, Aileen,' I said. 'I love Ireland, but there the soft mistiness covers everything. Look at it here!' But what I really felt was that all this was too violently bright and cheerful. Every splash of technicolour seemed to deepen the darkness in me, my own dismal reality. I felt terribly out of place. I had no right to enjoy anything. I had left Mary in Ireland on the excuse of having to work; so work would be my only justification. I had no business sitting here on Aileen's back steps, looking down over the lawn towards the lovely stretch of water, a pond with reeds and ducks and swans, a local wildlife refuge. Oh, how Mary would love it here, and I'd left her in Ireland. Get up, I told myself sharply. You have to work, put things together, be busy, make the days count.

Late that afternoon, after Nannie had boarded the train for New York, we returned to my father's house. Aileen joined us after dinner, and we all talked and drank. After I'd put the children to bed Aileen and I talked – talked for hours, and stayed up far too late. And I drank far too much. I lay in bed that night with the room spinning around me, almost frightened to think how I'd feel when I woke in the morning.

The next day I felt terrible. Mimi came in to see how I was. 'I can't get up,' I said. 'I don't want to get up. Ever.' It was late, very late. The children had been up for hours.

Bonnie, Mark and Mary in Ireland (1973), when Mary was five months old *Carol Geltman*

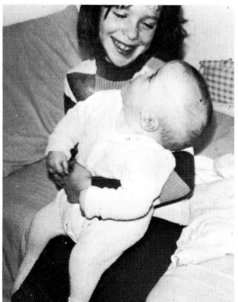

Mary, at nine months (1974), with her sister Bonnie *Carol Geltman*

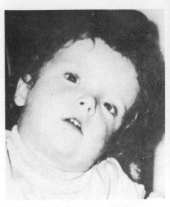

Mary's passport picture, taken in Ireland during my visits there, in 1975, when Mary was twenty-seven months old. *Below:* 'So-o-o big!' Mary and Bonnie, 1977 *Carol Geltman*

Bonnie and Mark with Mary (1977). Whose doll has her stroller, too. *Below:* Playing in a 'fort' built by Mark (1978) *Carol Geltman*

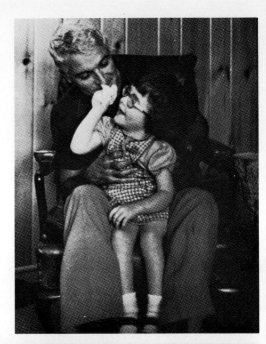

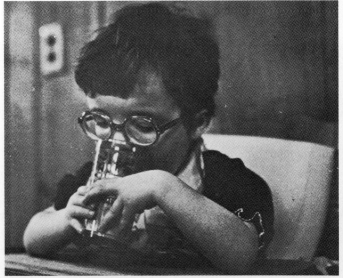

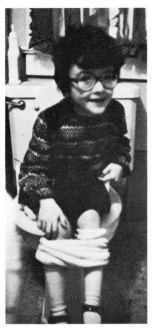

Far left: Tom and Mary (1978) *Carol Geltman*

Left: Mary, on her throne (1979) *Carol Geltman*

Below left: Mary, consumer (1978) *Carol Geltman*

Below: Mary, grocer (1978). In background, part of Priscilla the cat *Carol Geltman*

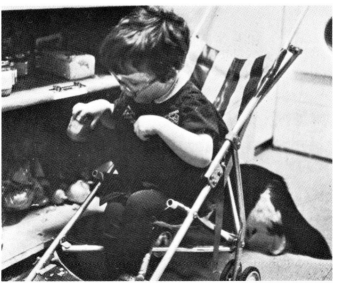

On the beach at Westhampton Beach with Mark, Bonnie and friends (1978) *Carol Geltman*

Right: Mary in her wheel chair (1979) *Carol Geltman*

Below: With Bonnie and Mark on the swing on Westhampton Beach (1979) *Carol Geltman*

Top: Mary (right) in one of her class photographs at St. Charles School, in Port Jefferson, N.Y. *Carol Geltman*

Centre: Mary (1979), six years old, doing leg flexing exercises with Bonnie and me *Carol Geltman*

Family group (1979) taken by Tom *Carol Geltman*

They'd had breakfast and lunch and were playing outdoors.

'Of course, dear. You're tired. But you'll feel better.'

'No. It's no good. Nothing's right now. It's the future. I can't face it. It's impossible.'

'Oh, yes. Yes, you can. You can, Pat. You must! Nothing is impossible, dear.'

'You don't understand, Mimi.'

As I half sat up in bed, the hangover began to seem a trivial surface disturbance. It was anger that was boiling and bubbling now under my freckled skin. Everything I didn't want to face was there, clear and real. Little Mary's life was my life, my responsibility. I lay back again, crying; ashamed of crying, covering my face with my arm, trying to stop. All my nights and days, all my future belonged to little Mary now. Forever. And not ever again to me.

'I know what you feel, Pat. One day at a time, dear, that's all.'

'That's it,' I cried. 'Every day. You don't see. You don't understand. You don't understand about Aunty Vi.'

'Aunty Vi?'

But I couldn't explain.

Mimi patted my back and left me, saying I would feel better. I got up half an hour later and spent another half hour in the bathroom, trying to erase the ravages of alcohol and tears. I kept splashing cold water on my skin, holding cold washcloths to my face. I stared at myself in the mirror, my eyes puffy, my whole face swollen and red as though I'd been in a fight. What was I? I was little Mary's mother.

Manhattan Nights

Manhattan, the island city – its towers and spires were tucked up into the night sky, looking from afar like fabled castles surrounded by an enormous moat. The smoke from a hundred thousand combustions hazed the prospect, making it seem as though mists were hanging on the battlements, making the towered city more fabulous, shrouding it yet further in mystery.

As a graduate student, I'd studied at Pratt University across the East River in Brooklyn, living one summer in a highrise apartment house near the campus. At night, in the summertime, I'd often go up to the roof with other students, and we'd look west and see the greyness of the city rising against the sinking sun. The city was always the mainstream to me, the place where you were put to the test, and sought your fortune; the place where the riddles were, and where you solved them. A place of magic and magical strange powers, of even stranger summonses and demands. Yet it was not here in this island city, after all, that the real riddle had been put to me, but on the shore below another city on an island across the sea. As the weeks and months accumulated, I felt more and more that I had not only failed to solve the riddle, I had failed even to understand it.

And I could not come to terms with my failure.

The children stayed at my sister's house on Long Island during late June and July, and on Fridays I, or Tom and I, would take the train out for the weekend. In August, Mark became sick with a lingering intermittent fever and would not get better, so we finally brought both children to Manhattan to live with us in the office where we worked, among the black steel desks and typewriters. The office was on East Fifty-Seventh Street, a large converted two-bedroom apartment in a luxury building in mid-Manhattan. It was not ornamental but functional, with plain white walls and dark wood floors. Only the entrance area, with its couch and chair and small table with split-leaf plant, gave a sense of living space – and perhaps the back bedroom which was Tom's and my office and had a couch, convertible into a double bed, and a reclining chair besides two large desks and bookshelves.

The two children managed to make themselves at home immediately. They were delighted with the novelty of life in an apartment building and spent time riding up and down the elevators and visiting the lobby to chat with the doormen and porters. They made trips to the basement and watched the people in the laundry room – nattily dressed bachelors, their briefcases on the floor under the big central table, tucking their Lacoste shirts and Bloomingdale's underwear in to the pink washing machines, while black and Puerto Rican maids piled clothing from the enormous dryers into huge plastic baskets.

The children found a back exit which allowed them to emerge on another street – it was a block-through building – and they made their way around the corner, sometimes stopping for iced cream cones as they continued their way around to the front entrance without crossing any streets. They passed an art supply store, two exotic restaurants, an antique shop, and a shop which displayed expensive gold bathroom fixtures in the windows. At another corner was a Schrafft's restaurant and around the corner was a store which sold rugs and drapery fabric to interior decorators. In the evening, we'd push two of the smaller desks together in the middle of the big room to make a dining-table. We'd turn off the overhead lights and use candles now and then to make the place seem more homelike. At first we made makeshift beds for the children from the cushions on the convertible sofa. Eventually we set up two simple cots for them. They always seemed to sleep well. Mark had carried Mary's bunny with him from Sandycove. 'I'm just saving it for her,' he'd say. He took it to bed with him every night, resting his cheek against it. They seemed not to mind discomforts. In fact I think these somehow made it all the more exciting for them, as long as we were all together.

Bonnie and Mark liked to stand at the window, looking south at all the buildings and lights, listening to the traffic muffled by the windows closed shut because of the air conditioning.

'How big is New York City?' Mark asked one evening.

'Oh, very big,' I said.

He sat at the window, cupping his hands around his face to blot out glare from the lights. He was still there half an hour later, staring out into the darkness.

'Would you like to see the city from the roof?' I asked him.

'Oh, yes!' he said. In a twinkling he was out into the hallway. We took the elevator to the nineteenth floor, then found the door to the upper stairwell. Few tenants ever used the roof, most of which was occupied by ducts and water reservoirs and the elevator machinery housing. I pushed open the door and adjusted the lock. We crunched on to the gravel and stepped over to a floor of boards along the edge, near the four and a half foot wall. Mark's eyes were wide as he leaned against the edge and looked over the city. The view was directly to the south – the Chrysler Building, the Pan Am Building, the Empire State.

Mark began to look cautiously down, first towards the building nearest us, then further down, to the street twenty stories below, where tiny cars, trucks and buses streamed along. He looked up again, to our left where the lights of the Queensborough Bridge swung gaily across the blackness. He glanced across the stretch of roof to the brilliantly lit Art and Design building, its pyramided storeys stepped narrower and narrower as they mounted to the top. All around us were lights, some yellow and warm, some cold white and bright and piercing. Then the many-coloured neon lights – flickering blues, rolling reds, flashing yellows and greens, and the tiny pinpoints of red warning lights set atop the tallest buildings. It was warm and humid, and the sounds from below reached our ears as a mighty hum of energy. Honks and beeps, screeching of brakes, gears, grinding metal – the cacophony of a summer's night. Suddenly it seemed to me that this intensity below and around us was one organic seething, not so much of intelligence as of yearning, of wanting – a kind of raw purposeful force reaching out and fashioning itself, in a glowing, flickering pulsation of desire. I breathed in the air, inhaling slowly. There was, apart from the myriad lights and the undulating mix of surrounding sound, a density of smell and taste and touch. The touch was in the air that moistened our skin, in the air's tangible feeling, in its temperature, its coolness on our necks, its dampness in our palms. The moisture gathered up the smells, presenting them for our special delectation and disgust. There were fumes from the subways and from the underground pipes that release their gasses into the lighter air. There was that sour, ever so slight smell of garbage, that acrid taste of metal pressing violently on metal. One could not shut out any of the given stimuli, but the single impression, overwhelming, simultaneous and kaleidescopic, was of sight and sound, smell, taste, and touch together. It was as though we were careening through the night on a carousel – with Mary on the opposite hub – a carousel brightly lit and booming with music, except that a carousel is a machine and what we were given here was a great giant living thing rooted in desire and becoming.

And I thought how always I'd only seen the surface of things.

'How long would it take,' Mark asked in an awed whisper, 'to fall all the way down to the bottom?'

'I don't know – I never tried falling like that.' I whispered back. How true. Was I to trust the carousel thing? Abandon myself to the movement? I remembered how, when I was younger, I liked to go and stand in the middle of some untamed field, near a lake or stream, edged by trees and heavy bushes, and let the total impression flood over me, taking in all natural reality, searching for some sense of the Creator God present in nature and beyond it. What I saw now was that the city was nature too, that all the human activity was nature – the same nature, but more complex, more radically akin to nature than nature itself. I felt I could reach out and gather the lighted blackness in my hands and hold it, vibrating with its sound, charged with its tastes and odours and compacted energy.

So, with Mark beside me, I stood there speechless for a while, until finally he began to ask his questions, and his questions about the questions, which demanded better answers than I could deliver. So we left and went back downstairs.

On another day in New York I felt again that sense of being caught up in a larger and more incomprehensible universe, behind appearances, beyond my notions. Two blocks from the apartment building where we lived and worked was a supermarket where we would buy food – two blocks east on Fifty-Seventh Street, at First Avenue. One evening I came out of the supermarket, turning west towards home, and saw directly ahead of me something I had never seen before: the sun as an enormous disc of red-orange, framed between the buildings on either side, a sun so filling the sky that it dwarfed the towers, miles distant, at the end of the street where the buildings seemed to converge. And the traffic, this noisy, smelly, haltingly slow caravan of traffic, was all moving into the huge flat circle suspended at the end of a street which seemed to exist now solely as a ribbon of approach to the great disc. It was a time when I wanted to be gloomy. My thoughts ran around in tight little dreary circles. By now gloom was a kind of profession with me. But this was so big, so brassy, so bold a setting sun that I had to laugh outright in astonishment – tiny me, inching my way across Second Avenue with my brown grocery bag.

One day I met Peggy McEvoy for lunch. She was the most unconventional friend I'd ever had. We'd been room-mates during our second year in college, before she went on to a career in public health. Though we'd rarely seen one another since, we'd been very close friends, and I'd always admired her verve and originality. I'd always felt at ease with her with no need for any pretence, no need to be on my guard. Peggy and I ordered huge spinach salads, health bread, and a bottle of red wine, and we talked about the past several months, about our husbands, our children, our work; about the future, and therefore about Mary. I told her how desperately unhappy I was to have a handicapped child, and how worried I was about her future and how terrified I was about what Mary's life portended for my own.

Peggy lifted her glass to mine, smiling wryly, and I remembered the dreams and plans whispered in the dark in a dormitory room after the bell sounded for lights out.

'I sometimes wish she would just go poof,' I said.

Peggy speared a deep green leaf. 'It's odd, isn't it, Pat, that just ten years ago, or even five, she'd simply have been a miscarriage? We know enough now to save babies like Mary. We can keep comatose people alive. We can keep people with incurable diseases from dying in peace. It's strange – '

'It is,' I agreed. Feeling again the winding tightness in my stomach, I poured each of us another dollop of wine.

An aunt and uncle of mine, who lived in Oklahoma, had become very interested in Mary. My aunt sent me a book, the best selling story of Karen, a freckled youngster afflicted with cerebral palsy; Karen's mother wrote lovingly of her daughter's struggle to attain independence. Someone else gave me a copy of Dale Evan's book about her little daughter, who had been born a mongoloid and later died. These were stories of such high-minded courage, such faith and hope, that they deepened my sense of my own wretchedness. Was there no one who had ever felt as I did?

As the months passed the grey airletter with red edges became a familiar item in the mail: Ann Burrows reporting on Mary's health; Mary's progress, how responsive Mary was. And she'd nearly always end her letter with something to the effect that she was sure that Mary would tell us how much she loved us if she could. I'd write back and say that we hoped to be on our feet again soon, but after many exchanges I found myself becoming repetitious and began to write more specifically about projects we were working on and what the older children were up to. Sometimes I'd send along an outfit for Mary. Nannie, who no longer lived with us but kept in close touch, was very generous, always mailing Mary things. I remember particularly a lovely dress with puffed sleeves and smocking, and another of white linen trimmed with lace, with a pink satin sash.

*

One night in New York in early September 1974, I woke suddenly in pitch darkness. At first I didn't know what had jolted me. Then I heard the phone ring and blundered down the hall to the anteroom. The phone was on a spindly metal table next to the couch.

'Yes?' I rasped into the mouthpiece.

'Is Tom there?'

'Yes – '

'This is Jack, Pat.' Jack was Tom's brother. 'Mother called here,' he said. 'Dad just died.'

'Oh, Jack! Yes, I'll get Tom!'

Tom was on the phone for several minutes. Then he stood up. 'Give me that number again, Jack. I'll call her right away.' He made a writing gesture in the air and I gave him a pencil and pad. He sat down again and wrote rapidly. 'Yes, Jack. I'm calling her now.' He looked astonished as he hung up. 'They were in a guesthouse in Limerick. They went to sleep. In the morning she found him next to her, dead.' Rubbing his head, Tom said, 'Don't you think I should fly over there right away?'

Tom left that evening on an Aer Lingus flight that would arrive in Ireland the next morning. Tom called early the next evening, his voice strangely not sad at all. His father and mother, travelling in Ireland, had just returned from Dublin, where they'd visited little Mary, had given her a musical pull toy, and had taken photographs. Tom was full of enthusiasm about the Irish ritual. 'It's beautiful!' he said. 'They didn't embalm his body. It's all very natural and simple. He was dressed in a white linen vestment and there were twenty minutes of prayers in the hospital morgue. Dad's body was taken to the church. The funeral mass is in the morning. He'll be buried in the graveyard where mother's family is buried, in Bruff.'

'How is she – your mother?'

'Still pretty bewildered. It was hard on her. But she'll be all right. She has all our relatives around her now.'

'Then it's good that you're there.'

'Yes, I think so. It was her decision to have Dad buried here. So I'm staying on to help her with arrangements.'

'She wanted him buried there?'

'Yes. Too complicated to ship his body home. Besides there is the family here, too. It's so much better. The graveyard is right next to the church. I wish you could see it – it's perfect. Mother's going to be buried there too. And you and I, maybe,' he laughed. 'And, by the way, when they visited The Cottage Home, Dad was quite taken with little Mary.'

I knew I was drinking too much. The old screaming would wind up, and I'd feel it gathering force, somewhere way beyond the horizon of consciousness, covered over most of the time by the clink and clatter of everyday doings. But this – it was like an 'ahhh' sound at first, then higher and higher, an 'eeee'. If I drank, the alcohol took the sharp aching edge off the screaming and it receded to a dull, long discordant echo. The scream was always there, in a darkness, humming like the sound of existence – the cosmic noise, but gone sour. In the night, going from waking to sleep, that hum would be there, like going underwater. When I'd step into some dark place, a closet, a cellar, it seemed to increase in intensity. When it would increase, gathering force and pressing upwards, I'd feel a constriction in my chest and my throat. When I dry swallowed, it was as though a lot of fleshy gears were meshing and shifting clumsily, forcing air downwards to pile up, adding to the pressure. But a glass of red wine, or better still of cream sherry – oh, that made a difference! For fifteen minutes the scream machine would disconnect. I'd feel limp and buoyant, sitting there on the black couch.

And then, to forestall the scream's winding up again, I'd take another glassful. I didn't even like cream sherry, but it was sweet and strong, tasting less like medicine than Scotch or gin, so I came to prefer it. And, as I told myself, I was only drinking wine.

One night when Tom was in Ireland with his mother, I was horrified to find I'd finished an entire bottle of sherry in a few hours. The result was a terrible headache, and soon I was violently sick. Worse than that, the screaming was more awful than ever. I looked at the clock. It was only ten. The children were asleep. I was alone with the long night stretching before me.

I'd been drinking heavily like this since the spring, finishing off a half bottle of sherry, an entire bottle of wine, maybe more, each evening. Sometimes it would be several stiff Scotches or gin mixes – whatever was on hand. I dreaded going to bed without Tom beside me. After I'd had this much to drink I could predict what would happen. I would lie there in the dark, sick and scared. Maybe I'd sleep fitfully for a few hours. Then about three-thirty I'd wake in a panic. That was the pattern.

Tonight I was throwing up. It was half a physical retching, half revulsion, self-disgust. Then came the screaming, louder and worse than it had ever been. I wandered aimlessly about the room, wringing my hands, gulping air. I had to fine someone to talk to, someone who could help. I felt I was likely to kill myself if I kept pouring this alcohol down my throat. My eyes were puffy, my face bloated. I thought I had probably already seriously damaged my liver. I was destined to die, I decided, and the idea seized my imagination. I put my hand where I thought my liver was, wondering how any organ could process all that alcohol. My liver, I concluded, must already be fatty and grey with disease. What would Tom do, if I died? I saw mental slides of scene after scene. The sad and weeping faces – Tom with his head in his hands, the sorrowful children in the care of sullen-looking women. And little Mary, alone.

Then I had an idea. In the apartment next to ours lived a doctor, a general practitioner in his sixties. He was unmarried, and his mother, who was in her late eighties, lived with him. He was a thin, austere man. With his unwrinkled face, he looked years younger than he actually was. We'd see him in the building several times a week, usually in the hallway or on the elevator, and he always asked about the family. I'd heard that he refused to accept any patient who smoked, and that he believed strongly in preventive medicine and good nutrition.

That night I sat heavily at the desk in the back room, deciding whether to reach for the phone. It was late – after ten at night. I decided I'd call him anyway. He'd examine me, and tell me if I were going to die, or whether I had so damaged my health that I had no future. So I picked up the phone.

'It's terribly urgent,' I said. 'I'm sorry to be calling so late, but if you could help me, I'd be very grateful.' I could scarcely talk.

He answered in a soothing, rather high voice.

'Mrs Collins? Yes, of course. Glad to help. I'll be right there.'

In a few minutes he was at the door, and I led him into the back room.

'It's me. I have a terrible pain – it's been going on a long time now – '

'Oh, I see.'

He had his little black bag with him, I noticed. I sat on the couch and he perched himself on the secretarial chair, his steel-rimmed glasses glinting in the light.

'I've had this recurring pain here and all around here – '

132

I moved my hands around my middle just above my waist, conscious that he was studying me. I felt foolish. If I were bleeding, maybe, or there'd been a swelling, or a bright magenta bruise – that might be worth the man's time. But to drag him over at this hour – to talk to a neighbour who thought she had a grey liver and who had a screaming going on inside her that wouldn't stop –

'You think you have a pain there. What is it like? Is it sharp? Stabbing? Is it a dull ache?' He asked his questions and waited.

'It comes and goes,' I said. 'But lately it seems to be there more and more. A dull ache, but a pressure building up inside.' My liver, I wanted to say – it's all grey and blobby with fat, and I'm really frightened I'm going to die because I've been drinking too much.

He felt my middle as I lay there on the couch, pressing his fingers around under my rib cage with slow steady firmness. Then he smiled. 'I feel nothing unusual. Everything is normal as far as I can tell.'

'I've been so worried,' I said, sitting up now, trying to seem casual. 'I thought surely I had something serious, like cirrhosis of the liver. I've been drinking a lot.' I continued on, fully aware of how ridiculous I sounded. But I'd built up a momentum of anxiety. I needed to confess, and so I told him about Mary.

'Oh, that's a shame,' he said. 'It must have been very difficult for you.'

'Yes,' I said, sniffling. But I was catching on to the idea that I was not harbouring some alien mass, and was so relieved I decided to confide further. 'I worry that I caused her premature birth. I was taking on too much.'

He sat there for a moment, looking at his shoes. 'You say that she was born at six and a half months?'

'Yes.'

'Well, it's no wonder she had difficulty breathing. The

lungs are not fully developed then.'

'Could I have prevented it?'

He held his hands open, palms up. 'No. No. These things happen all the time. And the parents always think they're responsible. I suppose that's normal. But we do enough things wrong, things that are really our fault. We shouldn't be taking blame for things we can't help. I'm surprised though – '

'At what?'

'Well, a baby born that early – maybe she was even younger, you know – is bound to have something wrong with it. Yet they pull them through.' He looked angry. 'Why do they do it? Why? I've seen the sorrow and anguish caused by babies that are deformed, or retarded, or who can't live without being hooked up to some kind of machine. It's not *fair*!'

I looked at him. I didn't think it was fair either. *Fair?* – I'd never thought there was any choice in the matter.

'You mean a doctor could have just *left* the baby there – ?'

'Perhaps,' he said.

I frowned, seeing what he meant. Perhaps, if she'd been born in New York, the doctors wouldn't have let Mary live. It would certainly have been easier to accept the death of a baby I never really knew than the deformity of one I knew very well. There would have been a little funeral, and she'd be a sad memory. The other children would speak in hushed voices about 'my little sister who died'. All very poignant, but we'd get over it – and go on, unencumbered.

The doctor told me to get some sleep. In the future, he said, if I must drink I should try not to take more than two glasses during an evening. When he left I switched off the light and the outer room was dark again. Through the windows, I saw buildings, but when I turned away I saw my little Mary's face. I turned to look again, thinking about the city out there, all the humming and stinking and yearning. A police siren wailed. Trucks rattled by and brakes screeched in the distance. My head ached. I still felt sick, but calmer. At least I'd be able to sleep for a few hours. I groped my way down the hall to the middle room where the two children were flung across their cots, covers loose, arms and legs outstretched. Yes, I thought, if modern medicine could keep a premature baby alive, why couldn't it provide a normal healthy child into the bargain, a child who could grow and develop like these two. *It's not fair*, the doctor had said. And years ago, as Peggy had said, Mary might have been a miscarriage. Maybe in another ten or twenty years, medicine would be able to prevent premature babies from suffering brain damage. We were caught in a medical parenthesis, weren't we, creatures of our own time and place?

The whining in me still high and persistent, I covered the two sprawled bodies and went to snatch what sleep I could.

'But Pat, you wouldn't unwish her, would you?'

'I can't now, can I?' I said. 'Maybe they shouldn't have pulled her through.'

Tom was back. We'd unpacked his brown bag and briefcase. Our debriefing session had degenerated into an argument about attitudes.

'What if she'd died? Wouldn't that have been worse?'

'Not for me, maybe,' I said slowly. '*You* don't have to *care* for a handicapped child. I do. Nothing's changed much for *you*.'

Tom didn't say anything, at first.

'Well, you could always get help,' he said.

'How can you say that? Tom, you don't understand. You think it's all so simple, that we can just hire someone.

Who? What kind of person? Oh, I just can't stand thinking about the future.'

'Don't then. Maybe that's the problem.'

'Be an ostrich, like you?'

'I wouldn't want her to have died, Pat.' He said it slowly, meaning it.

'But you don't want her here in this office, do you?'

'At the moment that's impossible. And she's fine where she is – '

'She should be with us. We're her parents. Her family. It's the first few years of life that count. The emotional attachments. The love.' That conviction or theory about the first few years was a favourite torture point with me.

'Well, we just can't – not right now.'

'Sometimes I think that I've botched things so, that I never want her back again – I mean, I'd rather have her in an institution, you know, a convent of some kind, and visit her there.'

'You would? God! You really are in a black mood.'

I was. I knew it. It was like feeding a fire, tossing in scraps to keep it burning. My black mood had begun to give me a perverse pleasure.

'We should never have gone to Ireland; I should never have let Nannie take over. And we should never, never have left her there. What was already a tragedy I've made much much worse.'

'You keep torturing yourself with all that. And me, too.'

'It is bad. What we've done is bad. Everything.'

'I've had enough, Pat,' Tom said, getting up and going over to his desk. I wandered out and saw in the darkness in the outer room, my face in my hands. It was awful, awful, awful. The scream machine wound tighter. I fixed a glass of wine, gulping it down in big swallows, waiting there in the darkness till the warmth began working its way around the screaming. Then I poured a fresh glass, and one for Tom, and carried the two into the back room.

'Here's a glass of wine before we go to bed,' I said, setting his on the desk. He had his feet up, his body tilted back in the chair, a book on his lap. His red reading lamp was on. The rest of the room was dark with shadows.

I took the cushions off the couch and pulled out the inner frame which turned the couch into a double bed. The sheets and blankets were already on it. I got the pillows from the closet. Soon I was ready for bed, and climbed in with a book, putting the empty glass on the floor

'Are you coming to bed?' I asked.

'Yes.' Tom was very quiet.

'You think I'm terrible, don't you?'

'No, I don't, Pat. I understand.'

Departures

It was the next night.

'Would you really want to put Mary, permanently, in some kind of institution?' Tom asked, testing me. He was propped up in bed against the big red pillow, the desk lamp swung out over his book. I was still awake, lying there, hiding from the light.

'Not really.' I reached for his hand.

'Good,' he said, squeezing mine.

'That way it would be harder. She'd be a stranger, and we'd have no relationship with her. Weekends we'd pick her up and bring her home. And then what would I do with her?' I imagined wheelchairs in the house, and awkward meals, and me bathing and dressing a stranger who behaved according to someone else's standards – a head nurse's, or a nun's. 'She wouldn't be *our* child. She'd be no one's.' I sighed.

'When she's older,' Tom said, 'she'll be at home. I can see that.'

'No institution?'

'No. What for? She'll be bright. She'll just need a little help. We'll find a way.'

I wanted to agree with Tom, but he sounded so naïve.

'You're glad she lived, aren't you?'

'Oh, yes,' Tom said, and smiled at me. You're really crazy, Tom, is what I felt like saying. You don't know, do you? But then it was better, wasn't it, that he felt the way he did? What if he thought that she'd be better off dead? What if he somehow blamed me? It happened – the parents turning on one another: man walking out on wife and family; man shooting wife and self. I loved Tom for his optimism, his happy-go-lucky going forward with no remorse about the past and no taking time to pick at scabs.

'I wish she were all right, Tom. I still do. I find it so hard to accept what's happened.'

'So do I. But we've got to take Mary as she is.'

'How could God do it? I just don't understand, Tom. I really don't.'

'God loves us. He loves Mary.'

'He sure has a funny way of showing it, then – an innocent little baby. What did she ever do to deserve those handicaps? Or the other little children – the blind ones, the ones born with organs outside their bodies, or the thalidomide infants, or the children maimed horribly during wars, their arms and legs blown off, the children incinerated in concentration camps? The napalmed children in Vietnam, the starving skeleton children in India? Even Ireland – what about the famines in Ireland, whole families dying by the roadsides?'

'It's a mystery. Look at Job. God's ways are not our ways –'

'That's a cop-out.'

'It seems so, I suppose.'

'Oh, Tom!' I was exasperated. 'I just can't put my trust in God. I want to, maybe, but I can't. It's too simple-minded.'

'Oh, Pat. You're tired. What can I say?' He sighed and patted my shoulder. I envied him his faith, trust, confidence, even his complacency. He willed things to come out right. But sometimes they didn't. I heard a siren sounding below, its shrillness breaking into the rumbling din below the window.

'I'm glad you think the way you do,' I said. 'But I guess I just don't have faith any more. Not in the God I grew up

139

with, whoever he was.' I blew my nose and lay there, my mind tumbling with images. If only I could turn it off. If only Tom would turn off the light. I felt myself drifting off, half listening to the city sounds.

In December, the month Mary was supposed to be rejoined with the family, we were still in the New York apartment, still living amid the desks, typewriters and bookshelves, still unable to take on the added burden of Mary. I'd sent another letter to Ann, saying we needed more time. But I felt awful, writing that. I did love Mary, I told myself; of course I did. But the mechanics, the practical day to day coping with her and her disabilities – that was the problem. I couldn't just bring her here and trust to luck.

On Christmas Eve we set up a tree, a very full but very small one, in the corner of the large room, strung it with lights and decorated it with ornaments from previous Christmases. The children had been attending the two-storey public school across the street. A play yard was thriftily set atop the second storey, and from our sixteenth floor apartment we could look down and sometimes see Bonnie or Mark running and hopping and jumping with the other children – bright specks above the traffic below. During the school vacation they spent their time looking at books or watching television or playing with toys around the tree. Their gifts had been small and inexpensive, but they'd been pleased with them.

'Will Santa Claus give Mary presents?' Mark asked.

'Of course!' I answered heartily.

'Does Mary still remember us now?' Bonnie asked. But I couldn't answer that question with the same conviction.

I'd bought Mary a puppet, a little cloth puppy with a red tongue. I'd wrapped it, put it in a jiffy bag and airmailed it to Dun Laoghaire. It was not expensive, and it weighed very little in the overseas mail. It had seemed a paltry offering for a little girl's second Christmas.

Tom's mother was with us for the holidays. I'd always been very fond of her. She liked being with people and, after Tom's father's sudden death, she'd gone back to work. She was a small person, tiny and thin and frail, and one day while she was at work in a large university architects' office, a messenger boy, rushing along a corridor, had toppled her backwards, knocking her legs out from under her. She fell like a bowling pin, with nothing to break her fall – crashing down on to a tile-covered cement floor, the back of her head bouncing against the hard, hard surface. She'd all but cracked her skull, and she was what she herself called a 'basket case' for a month or so. With a concussion so severe, it naturally took some time for the headaches and ringing in her ears to stop. But hers was a tough and durable frailness and she gradually recovered. For her the best thing about the accident was that she decided to retire, and consequently was able to visit with us, and with her elder daughter in Denver, for long periods. She was still not fully re-covered when she arrived in November for a holiday stay with us. But taking full advantage of our being in mid-town Manhattan, she began to regain some of her verve, going to church every morning, shopping, visiting old and new friends, involving herself in senior citizens' activities.

All our work still seemed mere wheel spinning. I thought of looking for a job, and made some serious gestures in that direction. But I was relieved in a way when nothing came of my efforts. For me to take a routine job wouldn't solve anything. Anything I'd earn would have to be taken out again to pay for child care. And the recession was still in full swing. People were being dismissed from jobs. On a single day one publishing company let a hundred people go.

If only Tom and I together could get a few projects going – that, I felt, would solve our problem.

I persisted.

'I'll get a job as a secretary – just as a typist – ' I'd say.

'It wouldn't help,' Tom would say. 'The money you'd earn would be a drop in the bucket.'

We tried to keep our problems from the children. They saw us working as we had always worked – the planning sessions, the ringing of the telephones, the busy type-writers, people coming and going.

Four days after Christmas, the children picked up their toys and carried them off to the middle room. We swept the tinsel from the floor, the office was back in business. It was then that Tom told me he'd decided he wouldn't pursue book development and agency activities so singlemindedly anymore. Instead he would write his own material. 'Fiction,' he said, and he went into the far room and closed the door. It was a remarkable thing to me that, despite all we'd been through, Tom had never become sour or bitter. I remembered a friend of ours saying how greatly he respected Tom for his grace under pressure. I used to think of that often, as I'd see Tom late at night, writing in his sliding longhand on large yellow green-lined legal pads. He'd keep on doggedly. He'd reach the bottom of a page and then flip it aside and start again at the upper left corner of a new sheet. I helped him with this, and with some agency and development work, pursuing leads that might turn out to be profitable.

This is what I did during the day. At night I would drink.

'When are you going to bring Mary over?' we were often asked.

'We don't know,' I'd reply. It was the truth. There was no likelihood at this point of our returning to Ireland. So I mounted a small campaign to gather information on places in and around New York where little Mary might go for therapy. I visited the government offices to find out if Mary might be covered under some programme or other. We were not poor, I was told, so we couldn't expect government assistance. I gathered brochures, letters and lists – a Mary folder. In a few weeks it was bulging; it soon became several folders, and then a section of a filing cabinet – engorged with newspaper clippings, books and brochures on hospitals, schools, special clinics and institutions, material from congressional offices on new legislation for disabled children. I couldn't really interpret most of this. I didn't know what programmes Mary might qualify for. I took out books on the handicapped from libraries. I built hopes on fact and hearsay. I called people who I'd heard had handicapped children, asking all sorts of questions. I visited a special education centre and spoke to the director about their programmes. I visited state facilities. I only half knew what I was searching for, and I could find no central agency for special education. America! I found it hard to believe that in all this rich country there was no central computer with appropriate data. I lurched from source to source as in a dream, groping blindly for bits of information which, pieced together, might make some kind of coherent plan for Mary. Where she'd go to school, I felt, would determine where we'd eventually settle and live.

We hung on during January and February and March. Nothing much happened. Tom continued his writing. I'd work, mainly on book ideas and proposals, until the children returned from school, when they'd be told to be quiet till after five-thirty – 'business hours'.

For their sake, though, we decided to move from the

city. At the beginning of April, my sister Aileen called to say she'd heard of a place for us to stay on Long Island. Tom's mother left us and returned to Chicago. We sold the desks, typewriters, bookcases, projectors, and even the fluorescent fixtures, and dismantled the office. We retained a small base in New York City – space rented from an art studio in the same building – feeling that while we renewed our energies we needed to maintain some kind of continuity with what we'd been doing. It was an address we'd had for ten years.

So in the spring of 1975 we moved to the south shore of Long Island where my parents lived year round and my sister Aileen had her summer house. We sent the two children to the local public school; for the three remaining school months we bivouacked at a motel in Quogue, a town whose name was a corruption of an Indian word meaning 'land that quakes and trembles' – a reference to the marshy flats along the shoreline. Appropriate enough, I thought at the time. Though we were away from the city, somehow the temporariness and unresolvedness of our situation kept me drinking. I *wanted* to stop drinking. I couldn't understand how I could keep on doing something so destructive – something that made me so sick, so tired, so depressed. The few moments of peace and calm, of induced artificial benignity – were they worth it? No, of course not. But still the anxiety would build up every day, and every other day I would capitulate. Just one drink, I'd say. Or just a small glass of wine. But then I often couldn't stop till I'd had far too much. There were times when I wouldn't remember anything from the previous night. Twice I had vague recollections of near accidents while driving the car. 'Mommy, you're always so tired,' Bonnie would say. 'Do you have a bad headache again, Moms?' Mark would ask anxiously.

But it was during those days that something happened

that marked the beginning of the end of my struggle with alcohol.

One May morning I was driving down a tree-lined sunlit street. It occurred to me, as it had in New York, that I was gone, done for. In the next instant what hit me with a startling clarity was the conviction that there was no hope for me in myself. I'd never be able to stop drinking; I would only get worse. My own efforts to stop were futile; the solitary pep-talks, the self-inflicted threats, the violent resolutions, the dietary regimes, the magic tranquilisers – none of these would ever work. Driving down that street, I was seized by the unshakeable conviction that I was *utterly helpless* to help myself. Whatever impulses I'd had to solve the problem myself, to redeem myself on my own, were all played out.

I gave up.

'God, God, God!' I breathed aloud, gripping the wheel, tears running down my face.

That was all I could say, but at that point it seemed that a barrier began to melt away.

In June we arranged to rent a condominium for the winter season in Westhampton Beach. Meantime, for July and August, we took a house on the north shore, in the town of Stony Brook, not far from St Charles Hospital in Port Jefferson. I wanted to get acquainted with the hospital and with the area before returning in September to the south shore. In the last year or so, there'd been some movement towards government funding for the handicapped, and we'd heard that St Charles Hospital had a very good clinic school Mary might be able to attend eventually.

The summer of 1975, my guilt at leaving Mary in Ireland was growing. I still couldn't imagine her with me, because I couldn't imagine being free enough to take care of her and couldn't imagine being able to find the right kind of person to care for her while I worked at least some hours of the day. I was stewing in a horrible despondency. Then, in late August, we began to receive a series of cards and letters from Tom's sister Florence, who had scooped up her four children and taken them off to Ireland to visit relatives there. Naturally enough she'd stopped to visit Mary. But she kept returning to see her, and began spelling out her feelings of dismay. She could not understand our having left our baby in Ireland. She kept raising the ante, enlisting her own children in the cause, representing her urgings as theirs. 'Jane and Cece and the boys don't understand why you don't bring dear Mary to live with you,' she wrote. The noise of her reproach was pitched higher and higher with each arriving mail. On her return she began issuing her bill of indictment – at first by further cards and letters, and then by phone. She levelled a series of bitter accusations in which she gave voice to my worst thoughts about myself. 'Of course we're going to bring her over,' I shrieked at Florence over the phone during one final call from her, from her home in suburban Chicago. 'But we have no arrangements made for her therapy yet. And who do you think *you* are, telling us what to do about Mary? Why don't you mind your own damned business?' She had problems of her own, Florence had, and she was driving me even deeper into despair by lecturing me about mine.

A Visit to Ireland

It was September and the children had returned to school.

'Let's go over to Dublin,' said Tom's mother, who was visiting is where we'd moved, at the condominium on the south shore. 'We'll see Mary for ourselves,' Besides, she said, she wanted to visit Dad's grave. Tom urged me to go with her; he would take care of the children while we were gone.

So Tom's mother and I left for Ireland. From a hotel in Dun Laoghaire, where the two of us had just checked into a small high-ceilinged room, I called Miss Burrows to tell her that I was there and would be coming right over to see Mary. As I walked up the hill to The Cottage Home, I was anguished at the thought that, though it had been fifteen months since I'd even *seen* Mary, the one thing I wanted to ask Ann Burrows was that she keep her there a little longer. As I rang the bell I heard in my inner ear the echo of Florence's sharp, accusing voice: 'How *can* you?' she'd said, over and over again. I knew too, that over and over again she'd said the same thing to Miss Burrows: 'How *can* she?'

The massive door swung open, and the same rosy-cheeked young woman who'd greeted me a year earlier stood there, smiling. Behind her, in the shadow of the long hallway, I saw Ann Burrows, her figure silhouetted by the light of a distant window, standing near the main stairway. Miss Burrows was holding Mary, and woman and baby shared the same shadow; they were one figure with two heads. I walked towards them.

'Hello!' I called out. 'Hello, Mary!' She seemed much

bigger, her head much larger and her hair longer, than when I'd left her here.

Mary looked at me impassively.

Ann, holding her, watched her solemn face and saw what I was seeing. There was no slightest sign of recognition in my little girl's eyes. I hadn't expected her to know me, but the reality of her stonily uncomprehending stare – cold, remote, detached, uninterested – over-whelmed me. I know what it means when someone says, 'It broke my heart'.

I reached out and touched Mary's face.

'Hello, there,' I said.

Mary made a little anxious sound, moving closer to Ann Burrows, afraid that I would try to take her and hold her.

'Well, what do you think of your daughter?' Miss Burrows asked cheerfully.

'She's grown!' I said.

Mary looked at me. She was wearing one of the little outfits I'd sent her. It had seemed so large when I'd packaged it, but I could see that it was really too small for her now. Miss Burrows carried Mary as we walked down the hallway, stopping at the kitchen. The people who worked there came over to say hello. They began teasing Mary, and for the first time she grinned and smiled. We went outdoors to the garden, where the infants were sleeping in their lined-up baby carriages. Aides sat on the benches with the toddlers, the older children darting in and out, some of them playing on the swings. We sat down on a bench and I took Mary and held her in my arms for the first time in more than a year. She sat quietly, watching the other children, and watching the faces of the aides Miss Burrows introduced to me. 'Mary's mother,' Miss Burrows kept saying, while Mary herself sat in a stranger's lap. When their lunch was ready, the little ones were brought indoors again. Mary sat in a low table in the smaller of two dining-rooms. A trolley cart was rolled in and the children were served their meal in plastic bowls. I watched as Mary, a bib tied around her neck, a spoon gripped tightly in her right hand, set busily to work to feed herself. 'She does very well,' Ann Burrows said proudly. 'We usually help her at the end. She has trouble getting up the last carrot or the other little bits – '

After lunch, as the time approached for the children's afternoon rest, we went up to the Peter Pan nursery, as bright and sunny as I'd remembered it. I brought Mary over and sat with her near a window, while the toddlers played on the floor and the aides fed the tiniest babies. I didn't know what to say to Mary. So after I'd held her for a while, I put her on the floor, watching her hitch herself around by her elbows, rolling over and over till she got where she wanted to go. At least she could roll over now. I picked her up again. She didn't seem to be able to sit up at all. I let her down for another roll on the floor. I saw that she was quite independent and determined, inching herself over towards a plastic toy on the floor, getting hold of it, rolling over on her back and holding it up very near her little face so that she could examine it. Another child approached her. She held the toy tight, her feet moving slowly as she made fretting noises. I picked her up, the toy in her hand, and sat with her again. I stayed through her nap. Later in the afternoon I bathed her, and put her night-clothes on her after supper. She didn't seem to mind when I left her to go back to the hotel.

I stayed in Dun Laoghaire a week, visiting Mary every day. Sometimes Tom's mother would accompany me, sometimes I'd go alone.

When I arrived one morning to see Mary in the nursery, she was with a woman, a pleasant brown-haired mother with a smiling face, a volunteer who often came to help with the small children. Mary was sitting on the woman's lap having her fingernails trimmed with tiny curved scissors. They sat by the window and the light caught in Mary's curls as she patiently let the woman take each tiny finger. Seeing this, I longed to hold her myself, to wrap her in my arms and to tell the little girl who suddenly seemed no one's child that she *was* wanted, that I wanted her – that I was her mother and had wanted her all along. *We don't want you to go away*, I'd said once long ago.

The next day I took Mary down to the main street to get a photograph made. When I could bring her home I'd have to have a passport for her. Getting the photo was something palpable, something to do with Mary's coming to join us, and I felt better being able to do that much right away.

One evening Ann Burrows asked me to stay on for a late tea with her. After Mary and the other children had gone to bed, we went into the large kitchen, and I watched as she prepared a grill – egg, sausage and tomato. We carried our trays into a high-ceilinged room across the hall from the kitchen. We sat down at the table there.

Miss Burrows was very quiet when I asked her to let Mary stay a little longer.

'But how long?' she asked.

I told her of my problems, assembling a picture of what might be available in America. I wanted to make sure to have everything lined up, I said. 'Let us get settled in this town,' I begged, 'and let me make sure Mary will have a place to go to for therapy.' At first she said nothing. The room was very still. For those of us who have lived our adult lives in apartment buildings and similar houses, there is something about being in a room with a high ceiling. Conversations seem more significant, silences more dramatic.

'There's no one else in the family who could take her for a little while?' she said at last.

'No.'

'What about your parents?'

It was a question she and others had asked me fifteen months ago. My father's health was not good, I said. And two of my sisters had new babies. Another had moved away to Ohio. It wouldn't work: they all had responsibilities enough already. I did not add that it would have been intolerably embarrassing for me even to ask. I wondered whether she could understand the special problems of nuclear-family Americans – each little unit as self-sufficient as a pioneer family in the wilderness. 'I'm taking care of arrangements for Mary's passport. I've got the photographs,' I said. 'I'll get her birth certificate from the registry and the passport application before I leave.' I was hoping she'd see these gestures as a step forward.

'Mary has so much love to give,' she said. It was true, and I thought of the adoring way the little baby had looked up at her – and not at me. 'Your sister-in-law wanted to bring her back to America,' she said, smiling. Yes. Tom's sister Florence would have brought Mary back, if she'd been allowed to. And Florence had told everyone just what she thought of our leaving Mary at an orphanage in Ireland. She had apparently even tried to start some kind of legal action. Tom, and Tom's mother, were as angry as I was at her intervention, which had a strong note of self-promotion in it. 'Motherlier than thou,' Tom had said.

'Florence was quite taken with her.'

'Yes, I know,' I said. But Florence had financial security, a spacious home, and nothing at all to do but raise five undamaged and healthy children. When Florence and her family had been guests at our large seashore home in New Jersey for a month during each of three summers before we'd left for Ireland, I'd grown fond of her and her flock. I'd also come to know her propensity for impulsive and dramatic gestures.

Ann Burrows told me that the day she finally left Ireland, Florence had come with flowers, bringing her children along again – as witnesses to my neglect and failure as a mother.

'But I told your sister-in-law that any decision about Mary's leaving here would be up to her parents.'

'She wrote and called us,' I said, my face flushed. 'But I didn't know that she'd seriously tried to get you to let her take Mary home with her.'

'Well, she talked about it. I don't know, honestly, whether she would have.'

I admired Ann Burrows for her clear-headed firmness. But in this tale of Florence's usurpation, my own poor opinion of myself was again confirmed. Miss Burrows knew the terribleness of my anxiety, I think, in having to ask for more time when I knew I should have Mary. But I hoped she also knew for certain that I had not abandoned Mary. My being there was proof of that.

While I was in Dun Laoghaire, I saw Marlene twice, the second time for tea in a hotel lounge. She looked the same, the dark eyes, the soft little ironic voice – but no smile now. 'Hi, there,' she said. 'How are you?' Very formal. She seemed serious and withdrawn, as though forcing herself to be cheerful. I asked how she'd been doing, and how her work was now. Was she happy? She shrugged. 'I'm never happy,' she said making an effort to be mysterious. 'No one is.' And then suddenly, her eyes hardened. 'Why did you fail?' she asked – a non-sequitur, it seemed. I couldn't quite understand her question. It wasn't the words, but the fierceness in her voice and hard look in her eyes. Not contempt but dashed hope.

'Fail?' I repeated, trying to formulate a response. But then Tom's mother came to join us at the table.

If there was a failure, it was one of the heart, I thought.

A Place For Us

I hadn't ever intended to get drunk on Thanksgiving Day. That fall, in fact, I'd been drinking hardly at all. Our financial picture had begun to stabilise, principally because we were no longer carrying the huge overhead that our larger business efforts had entailed. Tom and I worked hard. He was doing his writing, and handling substantial small publishing projects, and I was helping him, doing editorial and design work and agency correspondence. We had done well enough together to steady our small ship, and I'd decided I wasn't behaving like an alcoholic any more. All I'd take was an occasional glass of wine with Tom. I felt pleased that my drinking was again under perfect control. I felt so good about it that, at my sister Aileen's home on Thanksgiving Day, with the rest of my family gathered around, I felt I could easily afford to indulge myself in a Scotch or two. So I did. Two or three, and they were good ones. It was a lovely occasion – candles and flowers and all the silver, the huge turkey dinner, the festive spirit. My parents were there. Mary Ellen, my youngest sister, had come with her husband and their one-year-old son. Another sister, Terrie, spent a long time on the phone from her home in Ohio chatting with all of us. At dinner I had several glasses of wine – after the earlier whiskies. That must have been it. The last thing I remembered was walking around in the darkness out-doors, Tom talking to me quietly, as I insisted over and over again that I wasn't having any problem, and then going into the house and slamming the door in his face. But I was having a problem. I was loudly and angrily and inconsolably drunk. I had disgraced myself and frightened everyone, making the evening memorably unpleasant for all of them. I'd often enough confessed my shame at having left Mary in Ireland, and what I did now was demonstrate that shame by stripping myself of all decorum.

At home the next morning I couldn't get out of bed. I had a hideous hangover. I was bitterly remorseful. It wasn't until four in the afternoon that I emerged from our bedroom and tentatively made my way downstairs. Tom and the children were very polite, but I knew they'd been appalled at what I'd done. I felt cold all over. There were tiny snippets of memory – snatches of conversation, me yelling, shrieking and crying, blaming myself over and over; glimpses of bewildered faces: Bonnie and Mark not comprehending. And Tom's face, his lips tight, his eyes full of worry. Pat, you're your own worst enemy, my father used to say.

There was a woman once – an Irish woman who worked with my grandmother at Best & Company. Her name – call her Helen. When I was a little girl, while my father was away at war, Helen would come occasionally to a party at our apartment in Brooklyn. Not only would she drink too much, she'd cap her drinking by taking off all her clothes and dancing around the living-room, wrapped only in the sheer ruffled window curtains. I saw none of this – I was asleep whenever it happened. But my mother, aunt and grandmother and their friends, mentioning her name, would giggle and roll their eyes, and eventually I found out why. Whenever I met her she seemed very properly adult – stern and prudish, in fact. I couldn't imagine Helen doing a Helen.

I had used the alcohol not only to anaesthetise the pain I felt but to hurt myself. It was foolish – I'd already known that. But this was it. This had to be it, this time. Earlier I'd talked to Tom often about my drinking. He would try to help me and I'd fall flat on my face, and ask his forgiveness. Each time he'd forgive me wholeheartedly, and put his arms around me and encourage me. He was sitting in the living-room now, next to me.

'I'm terribly sorry,' I said.

'I know,' he said. 'It's all right, Pat.'

'I can't drink.'

'No, you can't. You just can't.'

'Help me.'

'I will.' And he put his arms around me again.

Winter and spring went by. Bonnie talked a lot about Mary to her new friends. Mark didn't, but Mary's bunny still kept him company in bed each night. There were setbacks, yet things went well enough generally. The four of us were happy – and happier still, when, after some eleventh-hour shopping for a home for the year ahead, we found and rented a place within half an hour of starting out on a house hunt.

In a resort town like Westhampton Beach, nearly everything is for rent in the summer, and most years there are last-minute opportunities. We'd heard of a carriage house in the village that might or might not still be free. On an impulse we drove there straight away. It lay on a quiet road, just off a dusty driveway on which a stone surface had once been packed. It was old but freshly painted – white shingle with maroon trim. There was a large cement terrace with an old tree growing out of it, a tangle of bushes and vines around its edge, and an ancient water pump. The main door was tall and wide, with an expanse of multi-paned windows. 'This must be the place,' Tom said. We knocked but there was no answer. I tried the door and it was open. We walked in and called. Still no answer. 'It's open,' I said. 'If they want to rent it, I suppose they wouldn't mind our taking a look.' We began walking through. The house was panelled in knotty-pine boards. 'It's not possible,' I said sadly, 'that with Memorial Day only a week away, the place would still be available.'

'Maybe it is,' Tom said. He opened a door to a small room off the living-room. 'Look, this could work as an office.' It had closets and a big built-in chest of drawers. There was a huge kitchen – occupying nearly half the first floor. Across from a bathroom a steep stairway led up to a second floor where there were four rooms and two baths. There was a tiny bedroom that would work well for Mary – cheerful, with a south-western exposure. The house was charming! There'd been a New York telephone number posted on a tree. We went out and I jotted it down. Just then across the driveway to our left, a tall man leaped through the hedge and called out to us. Tom waved to him.

'Is this the carriage house that is for rent?' Tom asked.

'Yes,' he said.

'What's the rental?'

He named a figure, saying it was for the summer.

'And year round?'

He gave the same figure.

'What's your best price?' Tom asked.

He named a slightly lower figure.

'We'll take it, for the year,' Tom said, and offered his hand to the somewhat startled man. He seemed delighted to have us. He was a genial fellow, a lawyer with a practice in New York. He and his wife were out for the weekend in their house across the driveway. We walked over and Tom gave him a cheque. After a quick drink (just soda for me, thanks) we were on our way, delighted with our discovery, and especially pleased with the speed with which we'd accomplished the transaction. Next day we were back again, unloading our belongings, assigning rooms to the children, reserving the small room for Mary. It was the first time, I felt, we could make deliberate plans, really imagining her with us. Not that there'd been a day or an hour when I hadn't thought of her – just that I had no direct emotional tie with her nor she with me. I'd come to feel I'd already failed her, and that I'd never be able to make it up to her.

I resolved to try to ignore such fears, and began constructing a fresh picture. I imagined Mary sleeping in the crib which Mark had used and sitting in his high-chair. I took a box of infant toys from storage in Mimi's basement and brought them to the house. I unpacked the boxes that stood in the hallway, and stacked the linens in the second floor closet. I was happy that we were settling down in this pleasant new place, and happy that it was suddenly June.

It soon became apparent that we were not the only inhabitants of the carriage house. During the winter the place had been closed and the spider population had multiplied. Every corner seemed to have one of these noiseless patient insects presiding over its nearly invisible apparatus, which was, after all, designed as a trap for the dried bodies of moths, flies and beetles. Coming downstairs in the morning I'd brush past webs. I'd reach the ground floor, swiping at my face and lips, and running my fingers through my hair. But the mice were the worst problem. They came from outdoors through crannies we could never find. None of us ever saw or heard one. But there was unmistakable mouse dirt on shelves and in drawers and on the tops of the refrigerator, oven, stove and counters. We had to rewash all pots and pans and cutlery before each use. That the stuff turned up in the creases of paper packages of food was particularly unnerving.

'They're all around – the mice – and there's not much you can do about it,' said the owner's handyman, a stocky decent man in his late sixties who looked after the grounds and did repairs. 'You've got to keep everything covered up,' he said, shaking his head. 'Use cans, or jars, or those canisters.'

'What about traps?' I asked. But I suspected he had as little liking for emptying them as I had.

'Why don't you get a cat?' he said. 'A good mouser is what you need.'

And so, several days later, through one of Bonnie's friends, we acquired a fierce, long-haired black and white female cat, and named her Priscilla after a British lady we'd met. Though Priscilla had an air of nobility, she also knew her obligations. She would mince and strut about, her tail waving like plumage, inspecting the rooms, sidling against a wall, stroking the back of a chair, patting and straightening and rearranging small objects. She seemed to assume that the clearance of pests was a natural accompaniment to her taking possession of her domain. She swished even into the spiders' corners, and when she emerged her fluffy tail would be festooned with webs. 'She's better than a mop,' Bonnie said.

The children liked to give her a ball of string to chase. That, to Priscilla, was appropriate play. They could pick her up and stroke her. But when they'd tease her, brushing their hands past her whiskers as she slept on the couch, waking her, she'd take umbrage, raising her head and shaking it; her paws would fly out, claws extended. She'd scratch. And she once badly bit the hand of an overnight visitor who'd had the temerity to introduce two alien kittens into the household. We bought a beagle for the children. It departed after only a few days, driven away by Priscilla's jealous wrath.

There was a regal ease about her patrols. She'd sashay

into the kitchen and, if there were a cabinet door open, she'd disappear inside, stepping delicately and as noiselessly as possible among the glasses and plates, the pots or canned goods (everything was below – there was no upper or wall cabinets) and re-emerge minutes later from a connecting cabinet door. She disposed of our mouse problem in a few days.

Priscilla was circumspect about the good order of her realm. Only once did any of us see her with a mouse. The children saw one she'd captured in a closet, and was willing, though not particularly anxious to display. In her insouciance, she couldn't be bothered showing mere mice, although when she was policing outdoors she did trot the odd rabbit or bird up for presentation. At night, if Tom were away, she'd come in to the living-room, her strangled warble of a meow raised at the end, like a question, on a higher note. Then she'd jump up next to me and lie down. If I were in the office, she'd jump on to the desk, arching and circling warily, and then settle herself down on whatever papers I was working with. It was the warmth of the goose-necked lamp on the papers that seemed to make that particular spot attractive. But I always took this as a kindly gesture, too, a mark of her special favour. She was preparing, she wanted me to know, to go to sleep where she could keep me company. She'd yawn and lay her head down. We'd stare at each other, Priscilla's ears twitching, waiting for me to say what I had to say. 'Come on old girl,' is what I had to say. I'd pick her up and put her on another table, under another lamp, on top of newspapers. She seemed inordinately fond of newspaper – the odour of ink, perhaps.

Priscilla's languid presence reminded me of the new peacefulness in our lives. The days of my crazy drinking were over. The deep anxiety was gone. Her slitted cat eyes would watch me lazily as I entered a room where she'd enthroned herself, and the eyes would gleam and flicker as she'd turn her head away again. There was nothing of any great concern, certainly nothing to get upset about, the cat seemed to say. All is well, everything is in good hands; it always has been, you know.

Mary Comes Home

Tom was under contract to write a political book. He left for Georgia in mid-June. A few days afterwards I received a letter from Ann Burrows saying how glad she was to hear that we were settling into our new house and that she hoped we'd be able to take Mary soon. I replied, saying yes, of course; we had some money for her trip and I'd send it to her as soon as I could. Then on 2 July, in the morning, the phone rang – Miss Burrows calling to say that she could bring Mary over herself, that there was a bank strike in Ireland and because of the delay in processing cheques, she could buy plane tickets now but wouldn't have to pay for them till later. We could reimburse her whenever we wanted. In fact, she said, she'd booked a flight and would be arriving with Mary the day after tomorrow.

'You're coming,' I said dumbly. 'Here? With Mary? Well, that's wonderful!' But I felt as though I'd been struck by a huge hand between the shoulders.

I was in the kitchen, a big tall-ceilinged room, originally a stabling place for horses, with two small windows high up. It was cut in half by a long counter, extending through the centre of the room like a peninsula, as Italy juts into the Mediterranean. The sink, stove, oven and refrigerator were to its left, and an area with a table and chairs to the right. The phone was on the wall opposite the end of the counter, to the left (in North Africa, so to speak). I made appropriate sounds of welcome, hung up the phone, went over to the counter and leaned on it, one elbow at Naples, the other at Rome. Because of the expanse of white counter the kitchen was always bright. There was a sweet scent, a new summery freshness in the air coming through the open windows. The trees, gently bowed by a breeze which fluttered their leaves, scattered and softened the light coming in the wondows.

'Wonderful!' Tom said when I phoned him later in Georgia. 'Our Dublin girl is coming home.'

The past was over and done with. Mary would be back with us in two days. I felt dread – and exhilaration.

We rose early the hot sunny morning of Mary's home-coming. On the long drive to Kennedy airport I was in a fog, my head full of distractions, my imagination running wild with possibilities. What if this were to happen, what if that? But I felt elated, too, as we sped along.

Kennedy International is a kind of pinball machine among airports – an organised chaos of bright signs and coloured dots and flashing lights along snaking roadways feeding the scattered terminals. Swinging right and left along the lanes and ramps, dipping under bridges, following the lights and signs, we wound our way around down the access road. The coin was spent, the plunger pulled, the ball was loose. There was no turning back. This is right, I said over and over again. This is good. This is what I want. I'd make it all up to Mary. I'd go forward, bash on ahead, blindly maybe, but I'd keep going on and never again hang back or hesitate. In the automated parking lot the turnstile pedestal spat out a ticket stamped with the date and time. The lot was vast and our space far from the building, so I had the children memorise the lane letter. We trekked through the lot, crossed the road and walked into the low glass and metal International Arrivals building.

We went upstairs to the balcony overlooking the counters of the customs area below. Down there the doors opened and closed again and again, until finally Ann emerged from a wave of travellers, calmly pushing an umbrella stroller occupied by Mary. Ann's pocketbook and navy raincoat were slung over her shoulder, and in her free hand she carried two bags. Mary, at three years ten days, was bigger and longer than ten months ago, but with the same round face, light reddish brown hair and white skin. She was wearing a little cotton dress and red sandals and was sitting back comfortably. But there was something about the inertness of form slung there in the stroller that bothered me. Her face had no expression. All around her was the bustle, the redcaps trotting back and forth, the thronging crowds, the squeals of recognition and shouts of welcome. Beyond the glass doors was the wheezing and honking and grinding of traffic. All this excitement, yet Mary was impassive. Her head lolled to the side, her arms were limp on her lap, her legs dangled from the stroller. I ached as I watched her.

We went downstairs. 'There she is!' the children cried. But something clutched at my insides and I was appalled to feel, despite all my resolve, the winding up, deep inside me of the phantom screaming.

I smiled and waved a shaky hand. I wanted Mary to smile and reach out to us and laugh. I wanted to gather her up and kiss her.

'Mary! Mary! Hello! Do you remember us, Mary, Mary?' Bonnie chanted as she and Mark bent down to the stroller, their faces full of excitement. Bonnie was ten years old now, and Mark seven.

'Hello, Mary,' he repeated. 'Mary, do you remember us?' Mark kissed her on the forehead, shyly patting her hair. 'Do you? Do you?'

'We're going to your house now!' Bonnie said. 'Aren't you glad? Mary?'

Mark stood up. 'She doesn't remember,' he said.

'No,' Bonnie said. She suddenly looked as though she were going to cry.

I hunched in front of the stroller and looked into the round white face. 'Mary!' I whispered. 'Mary!' If only, I thought, there were some hint of recognition – anything. But she was too young, it had been too long. And I had no right to a response from her.

'How big you are,' I said, stroking her white arms, thinking how doll-like she still was. She moved her arms restlessly and looked up, twisting her head in an effort to see Ann Burrows.

'I'm here,' Ann said cheerfully, as she leaned forward. Seeing her, Mary seemed relieved. She settled back, willing now to tolerate our chattering.

'She was sleeping – I don't think she's quite awake yet,' Ann said.

We gathered up the bags and left the building. Leaving them at the pick-up island, I raced across the roadway to the parking lot. I thought about Mary being here in New York, my little moon-faced child. Mary, Mary, quite contrary, whose garden grew no memories of me. My legs pumping, I reached the distant car, fumbled for the key, swung into the seat, which was hot from the sun. The air conditioner wasn't working. I began to sweat. I opened the windows. I drove through the exit lane, handing up ticket and money to the uniformed attendant. Belling and jangling like a metal ball as I went through the raucous machine, winding through each intersection, I sped around the loop, finally arriving at the island where Bonnie and Mark were waiting with Ann Burrows and little Mary. I pulled up and went around to get them settled – Mark in front, Bonnie in back with Ann, Mary on Ann's lap. We eased into traffic which bounced us off on to the roadway leading from the airport, away from its odour of jet fuels, its signs and lights, its maze of roads, lanes, connecting strips; its overpasses and ramps, and the flatness of it all under the big stretching dome of sky. I found the expressway and headed northeast away from Kennedy.

In the rearview mirror Ann looked bright and eager, her fresh face smiling, her air self-confident. What made her seem so like a girl herself? It was that Irish complexion of hers – petal-like, smooth and soft, highly coloured; and something childlike about her – simple and uncomplicated and good. Our country had to be strange to her. She'd never been here before. We opened the windows, the air rushing along into the back of the car. For the first time Mary seemed to react and respond as she felt the sweep of air feathering her hair, pressing on her face, forcing her head back. She laughed and so did the other children, and Ann laughed too. They began repeating rhymes and singing songs and Mary kept on laughing. It was a bright blue kind of hot day, the sun glinting off everything.

The highways unfolding in neat strips ahead of us, we were home, it seemed, in no time. In the house we went upstairs to put Ann's and Mary's things away. Ann would be here for a month, sharing Mary's room. The rest of us went downstairs to wait for Ann and the little one. 'I don't think Mary is going to get used to us!' Bonnie whispered to me. 'I don't think she likes us. What are we going to do when Ann leaves?'

'She'll get used to us,' I said. Inwardly, though, I was as worried as Bonnie.

When Ann and Mary came down again I sat with Mary on the couch and she seemed resigned to the idea of my holding her. I rubbed her little legs and her back and smoothed her hair – gestures, I hoped, which might magically help wipe away the two years' separation. I'd bless her back into our midst by the action of my hands.

Ann sat next to me. 'Well, you're back with your family,

Mary – your Mommy and your sister and brother,' she said earnestly. 'And soon Daddy will be home to see you!' She spoke slowly, her attention fully concentrated, soliciting Mary's reactions, receiving her tentative responses with respect. Mary gave her that wide smile I'd carried so long in my memory – the smile that plumped her cheeks into little apples and gave her face radiance. Mary stretched her arms to Ann, anxious to go to her.

I lifted Mary lightly from my lap. 'Ups-a-daisy,' I said, and nonchalantly gave her over to Ann. Clutching at her blouse, Mary settled herself into her lap. I caught Bonnie watching me, a wary look in her eye. *What have I done?* I thought. Would I ever receive Mary's trust and love? What shall I do? How shall I handle her? Would she always be just a little apprehensive about me, feeling that in leaving Ann Burrows she had left her real home, where she felt safe, loved, secure?

'Baa, baa, black sheep/Have you any wool?' Ann began, and Mary listened with rapt attention while Ann recited all the verses. 'More?' Mary said, in a low soft questioning voice. It was the first time I'd heard Mary say anything beyond 'no' or 'car'. Ann began another rhyme – 'Mistress Mary, quite contrary' – in a voice that combined authority and melody. 'Again?' Mary said, gazing up at her adoringly. When she'd reeled off a succession of nursery rhymes, one after another, Ann turned to Bonnie and Mark and began giving them riddles. They were delighted and she soon gained their rapt attention, too. But even while she carried on word games with them, she managed to keep talking to Mary, directing her attention to Bonnie and Mark, to things in the house, to the trees and garden outdoors.

Bonnie, who sat next to Ann, kept watching little Mary. Finally she asked to hold her. 'Your sister Bonnie wants you to sit on her lap. Is that all right?' Mary nodded, her face upturned to Ann's. Bonnie glowed as she took the child, wrapping her arms around Mary's waist, and bending her head down to rub her cheek against Mary's hair. 'You're back with us, you're back with us!' Bonnie kept saying, and I thought of all the love and attention Bonnie had lavished on Mary during the ten months of her life at Sandycove, of Bonnie carrying her, feeding and cajoling her, playing with her. Mary, who had worshipped her then, was not very responsive now. Bonnie glanced at me anxiously. Mark fell from time to time into a curious silence. His enthusiasm had been high all the way to the airport, but once we had collected Mary and Ann, the excitement ended for him. In the car on the way home he'd been quiet and aloof. Except for the rhymes and games, he seemed bored and restless. I smiled at him, and received a black look for my pains. He frowned, his lips pinched up. Disapproval? Disaffection? Something.

'What's wrong?' I asked. He was sitting cross-legged on the rug.

'Nothing,' he snapped, darting a frowning glance at Ann Burrows.

'Well, tell me later,' I said. He turned away quickly, his fingers picking at a tuft of carpeting.

After dinner Tom called from Georgia. He was full of questions about Mary.

'Does she seem happy?' he asked.

'Oh, yes,' I said.

'Are you glad she's home?'

'Yes.'

'I wish I were with you. I really do.'

When we'd finished, he talked to Ann and the children. He'd be working there, he said, for two more weeks, and then he'd go to Texas to finish the book.

Several times that night, Mary woke crying. Each time I

heard Ann get up, walk over and whisper to her. It was a closed circle, her relationship with Ann.

Mark's behaviour worsened the next day. In the afternoon I asked him to tell me what was wrong.

'I don't like her!'

'Who?' I asked.

'Her.' I felt an icy gust in my stomach. *He didn't like his little sister!*

'Mary?'

'No! That person. *Her*,' he said savagely.

'Ann Burrows?'

'Yes. Her.'

As far as I could see, none of what Mark felt about her was due to anything Ann had done or said to him. At least not initially. Mark had begun by refusing to answer when she questioned him, and by avoiding her eyes when she spoke to him. He'd made excuses not to go upstairs and retrieve something she needed for Mary. Last night he'd helped himself first when food was passed at the dinner table. Today he'd been stomping up and down the stairs; he'd turned on the television set while we were talking; he'd interrupted us continually. He'd used foul language gleefully, made gestures at Ann behind her back, and even deliberately slammed doors in Ann's face.

'But why don't you like her?'

'Because.'

'That's not a reason.'

'Because, that's all. Just because.'

'There must be a reason,' I said. 'Look, Mark, Miss Burrows is our guest. She's been like a mother to Mary. When Mary needed to be taken care of, when she needed to keep on going to the clinic in Ireland, Ann was there to do it. I like Ann very much. Daddy and I are very grateful to her. Mary loves her.'

'I don't.'

Ann had at first successfully ignored Mark's barrage of unpleasantness. But it was so unremitting that today she finally began to react – with gestures Mark was quick to pick up; an expression of disapproval on her face, a favouring of Bonnie in conversation. Mark seized upon Anne's reactions to his outrageous behaviour as justification for it.

'She doesn't like me, that's all.'

'Oh, Mark.' I said. 'If you're going to be so rude – really rude – then you can't expect to have someone smiling at you all the time. For heaven's sake!' I continued to talk to him, questioning and probing, but my inquiries yielded nothing. He was not only resolutely tight-lipped: he was oddly righteous.

'She's mean to me.'

'You're mean to *her*,' I began. But it was beginning to sound a little like a barnyard quarrel. At the moment I couldn't deal with him on a rational basis. So I'd wait and see what developed.

'Ann,' I said later, 'I hope you'll forgive Mark. I don't know what's wrong with him.' I could see that Ann was not at all pleased with his antics.

'He doesn't like me,' she said simply.

'But I don't know why. I don't know what's going on in his head.'

'Jealousy, perhaps. It's hard for him to move over now.'

'I wonder? Well, I hope he gets over it soon.'

During the weeks Ann was at the house, Mark seemed to mellow. Though he refused to talk to me about her, he became more polite and civil. It wasn't till two and a half years later that I found out what had really been bothering him: He'd made up his seven-year-old mind that Mary, in Ireland, was to have been magically cured by therapy under Ann Burrows' supervision. But Ann failed to look after her properly. So he'd conceived a punishment for Ann suited to that crime.

'She can say our names!' Bonnie announced the second evening. I was in the kitchen fixing dinner. 'Come quick,' she said. I saw the look on Mary's face – so full of pleasure as she repeated it in her faint breathy voice. 'Bon-nie,' she said. The last syllable was hard for her. She had to squeeze it out, with effort. 'And Mark,' she said, when Bonnie cued her by pointing at him. 'Mock' is the way she pronounced it.

'When will you bring Mary to see us?' my father had asked when he called one morning shortly after she'd arrived. He and Mimi had only seen pictures of her.

'We'll be there in fifteen minutes,' I said. But Mary looked at me warily as I announced the trip. 'Car,' I repeated. She was still suspicious. 'Going bye-bye!' I said. 'In the car.' Finally, a faint smile.

When we arrived my father was at the door. I lifted Mary into the stroller and straightened her little skirt. 'Here's Papa,' I said. He hurried to meet us, a big smile on his face. In all the green light from the trees Mary's white skin seemed to gleam, her curls stirred by a breeze. 'Well!' he said, and then went suddenly quiet. When his eyes met mine they were filled with tears. 'She looks so much like your mother,' he said in a gruff voice. He turned to her again. 'Hello, Mary! Hello!' he said. And then my stepmother Mimi called. 'Come in, come in.'

Indoors Mary sat like a doll, almost inert, as she looked around at Mimi's crowd of plants and flowers. We all talked to Mary at once. 'You're such a pretty girl,' Mimi said. 'And such a pretty dress! We're so happy to see you!' My father sang, 'For it was Mary, Mary,' waving his arms like an orchestra leader. Mary sat there with unblinking eyes. Yet it didn't seem to me that she was bored. There was something about the *way* she didn't move, didn't speak, didn't do anything, that seemed good and right. She was dispassionate, but as though absorbed in the scene around her. Yet why, if she was registering it all, did she give no hint of what was going on in her mind? Was she following clues, like a sleuth, carefully constructing and adjusting theories? Or was she judging us in some way?

Both my father and Mimi noticed her silent scrutiny. 'I wonder what she's thinking,' my father said. 'I wonder how much she can understand.'

'Her intelligence? I wonder about that, too,' I said. Mary, still solemn as a Buddha, was patting my hand. 'I think she's happy though.'

'Oh, Pat,' Mimi said. 'How fortunate you are that she's been so well cared for!'

After that I drove to the supermarket. Mary sat in the upper basket, gripping the cart handle, while I picked cans and bags and boxes from the shelves and put them in behind her. Her head lolled to one side, and she kept falling over to the left or lurching forward. Shoppers glanced at her pent-up little figure – staring, averting their eyes, then staring again. The stares didn't trouble me because Mary seemed content. I had my theory that she was absorbed in her work of observing everything. When she had to rest and couldn't focus any more, she'd just sit back limply, looking off into space. Then she'd perk up – her body stiffening, her fingers moving restlessly, her eyes blinking – subtle signals that she was *on* again.

Mary continued to watch us those first few days at home. Sometimes, when she was sitting in the car, she looked like a little guppy – her torso and limbs were so small in comparison with the large head. Her dark eyes stared out of whiteness, and their gaze was both intense and impersonal. More and more, despite that impassiveness, that silence, that stolid quality, I had the impression that something was going on. Energy was being spent, but in an inward, not an outward direction.

'But how much can she understand?' I asked Ann Burrows. I had steeled myself against the announcement I expected. Mary was retarded. I'd already accepted this as fact.

'Oh, well! I don't think your daughter's any genius. But then again, I don't think she's a dummy, either.' Though she said this firmly, it had no effect. My convictions were formed, and that was that.

Mary cried every night for the first week. Ann would put her to bed and we'd all go in to say good-night. Ann would stay with her a few moments longer, then say, 'Good-night, Mary. Have a good sleep.' She'd leave the room and join us downstairs. Mary would start in, crying and screaming, her screams growing stronger and stronger. I cringed, remembering Mary as a colicky infant – the long hours, the long terrible nights when she would wake and scream and scream.

'Do something, Mom! She's crying!' Bonnie said.

'Leave her,' said Ann. 'If you give in to her, she'll do it every night.' After a while those first nights, Ann would go upstairs, stand at the foot of the bed and speak to her softly. She'd ask Mary whether anything was the matter, she'd say that it was night-time and that she must go to sleep. Then Ann would leave and come downstairs again. By the end of the second week Mary was going to sleep without crying.

'Don't be bold!' Ann would say to Mary, when she'd be making undue demands. This was an Irishman for 'Don't get fresh'. Mary had a certain imperiousness about her. 'Do you know what I think?' Ann said once when Mary was being outrageous. 'I think she's a bit of a *madame*.'

'Oh, yes!' I said. It was partly the way she'd throw her head back – a sign of her disability, of course. But at the same time she'd wave her arms impatiently, draw down the corners of her mouth. She'd say 'No, no!' when not getting her way.

There was a paradox about Mary. She was strong-willed and determined and even bossy. Yet she was utterly dependent and defenceless. One hot and humid day we went to the beach, drawn by the bright sunshine and the sound of the sea. A half mile away as the crow flies, the beach was a mile's drive. When we got there we set up Mary's stroller and trekked through the broadwalk pavilion towards the ramp which led down to the sand. 'Let me push!' Mark said, and gleefully took hold of the stroller and stomped down the ramp while the rest of us trailed behind. Reaching the end, Mark pushed the stroller off the wooden ramp, then kept on pushing, expecting it to roll forward on the sand as it had on the ramp. But its front wheels sank in, and the stroller toppled out of Mark's control, so that only the rear stripes of the stroller canvas could be seen, and two spinning wheels. Mary's face was buried in the sand. There was no sound from her. Mark looken stricken. Frantically he grabbed at the handles, crying out, 'Oh, I'm sorry, Mary! I'm sorry! I'm sorry!' She'd fallen face first. She didn't have the normal reflexes or she'd have flung her arms in front to protect herself. Mark must have thought he'd killed her. Quickly we righted the stroller, and began wiping her sand-covered little face. She was shocked and indignant, her mouth drawn down at the corners, her lower lip trembling. Catching Mary up in her arms, Ann Burrows brushed her hair and laughed, calling her attention to the spread of sea and the children jumping and running in the surf. In a teasing voice she continued to distract and comfort her, and soon she was quiet and happy again. We carried her to the strand, where the children were playing. She squealed when the spray hit her, squealed again when she was dipped into the water. Mark was quick to improvise a sand seat for Mary, and he began building walls – to protect her, he said, from the waves. Several times she toppled over getting sand in her eyes and hair, but didn't seem to mind. She would roll off her towel and inch her way along the shore, stopping from time to time to roll over on her back, put sandy fingers in her mouth and squint thoughtfully at the sky. Then she'd stretch her arms above her head and slowly turn and roll off again, forgetting her helplessness, gaining again a measure of independence.

By the time Ann returned to Ireland, *madame* had made her peace with the New World.

On the Borderline

Mary now knew who we all were. She had particularly good rapport with her sister and brother, who behaved towards her like an indulgent aunt and uncle. They fed her and carried her; they played with her and tickled her and rolled with her on the floor; they gave her stuffed animals and brought her cookies and candy. Bonnie was eager to show Mary off to her friends. 'My little sister,' she'd announce. 'Yes, I *do* have a sister. She's handicapped. She's been in Ireland, getting therapy there. And now she's back!' They questioned me constantly. 'When will Mary walk?' they'd ask. 'What school will she go to? Will she be able to drive a car?' And from Mark, the blunter questions. 'Will she ever stop drooling? When she gets married will her children be able to walk?' By and large, they seemed to accept her as she was. Bonnie, who in Sandycove had been like a second mother to Mary — anticipating her needs, comforting her, feeding her and rocking her to sleep — took a special interest, singing to her, reciting rhymes, playing clapping games and peek-a-boo, taking her for walks, and helping in the daily regimen of exercises. Bonnie really believed in those exercises. She'd spend hours trying to get Mary to sit up by herself. 'I think she's getting a little better now, Mommy!' Bonnie would say. She'd bring her friends over and they'd tease Mary, sing to her, play records for her. Mary was especially fond of anything with pronounced rhythm. Most of our recordings were of classical music and she would brighten, clapping her hands enthusiastically, when she heard a trumpet voluntary or a piano concerto.

But when Bonnie delightedly said at the end of August, 'She's just the same Mary, Mom – only bigger,' I feared that it was all too true. My heart sank because what Bonnie was really saying to me was that Mary hadn't developed. There was a gap, one book said, and it just keeps getting wider as the child grows older.

'Don't you think she's changed?' I asked.

'She still laughs a lot and cries a lot,' Bonnie said. 'Not at night, thank goodness – '

'But don't you think she's a little bit brighter now?' I asked.

'A little,' Bonnie said. 'But she still can't sit up.'

'We'll keep helping her,' I said.

'I'm glad she likes us. I was afraid she'd miss Ann, and cry all the time.'

'If we love her, she'll love us,' I said. 'Love is like that.'

'I love her,' said Bonnie. 'I'm glad she's here.'

'So am I,' I said. And I was.

Late August, 1976: Here was Mary, in her blue and grey striped stroller, her hands lying loosely in her lap. Here was I, pushing her up the ramp to the ambulatory services clinic, bringing her to the clinic psychologist. Though I was curious I dreaded his examination. Mary didn't seem to be very intelligent. I'd been searching for evidence of mental development and hadn't found much to comfort me. She didn't know what before and after meant, or big and little, or yesterday and tomorrow. Everything seemed to be a *now* to her; she seemed to grasp things only in terms of their immediate use – food to eat now, a toy to play with now, a woolly blanket that would warm or scratch her now, a breeze that would blow on her now, books from the coffee table that might fall on her now; one of us to hold her or play with her or talk to her – now. When people would ask about her mental development, Tom would make his declaration of faith in her future and then revert to what we'd been told in Ireland – that she was really too young to test reliably. And he really didn't want to discuss my qualms. 'How do you know, Pat?' he would ask. 'Maybe she'll be a genius. We can't tell yet.' That seemed to leave me out on a limb as sole sponsor of the unpleasant idea that Mary was mentally retarded.

Mary sat passively in the stroller, guided by my damp hand. It was hot and humid in this empty place. It was the end of August, and most of the staff were on vacation. I pushed Mary down the incline, towards the small offices flanking the side entrance. As we walked along, Mark leaned over and began to pat Mary's head with his hand, smoothing her hair from her forehead, pulling her skirt down over her knees. He was as fussy as Nannie, who'd fussed over him for four years. Here he had the concentrated look of a sculptor, working from some ideal image in his mind, putting the finishing touches to his work. Mary began to raise her hands, in objection to all this touching.

'No, no,' she said.

Mark jammed his hands in his pockets. 'Okay! Look like a *mess*, baby!' Flushed and shining with sweat, Mary rubbed her face. She looked crumpled, as a side door swung open, and a tall bespectacled man with dark hair nodded to us, identifying himself as the clinic psychologist. We entered the room, a cramped enclosure barely large enough for the few small pieces of furniture in it. He sat down at a wooden desk against one windowless wall and motioned me to a folding chair facing him. Mark sank into another chair in the corner, slouching, chin on his chest, advertising his detachment from his sister. I sat on the edge of the chair, my right hand on the stroller handle. Mary was fretting, advertising her annoyance.

'I think she's tired,' I said, rocking the stroller.

'It's such a warm day,' the psychologist said. 'Right,

Mary?' He smiled, leaning forward to look into her face. She had no response. Pouting, she restlessly moved her right hand up and down on her lap. This was not going to be a success, I decided. The psychologist sat back – pulled the folder on the desk towards him and opened it. He glanced over Mary's records and swung his swivel chair around to face her. He pulled over a little table and set it level with her waist. I raised her in the stroller so that she could lean forward and put her hands on the surface. He seemed satisfied that he could begin.

'In Ireland they don't feel these tests are very reliable,' I said, as he picked up a wooden puzzle, each piece with a small hand peg for insertion and removal.

'I suppose they're not. You can get an idea.' He smiled. 'But sometimes we're proved dead wrong.' He put the puzzle board on the table in front of Mary. She leaned forward, patting it noisily. He lifted the pieces from their places and set them down beside the board. 'Let's see, Mary. Can you put those pieces back in there?' Mary looked at him blankly. 'Show me how you can put those pieces back in. Here, I'll show you.' He put all the pieces in, then took them all out again. 'Can you do that?'

Mary patted the table top, making no attampt at all to reach the little pegs. She began to drool, her little head swaying back and forth.

Mark gave Mary a look of disgust.

What a stupid exercise! I thought. We were just going through the motions. It was a formality – an empty ritual.

'Let's try something else,' the psychologist suggested cheerfully. He swept the puzzle into a box and took out some wooden blocks. Mary reached for a block but failed to hold on to it. Finally she got a grip on one, banging it on the table. 'Can you build a tower, Mary?' he asked, taking a second block and setting a third on top of it. He reached for a fourth block but Mary knocked her own into the three standing, toppling them. He picked them up and piled them again. 'See what I made? Can you do that?' Mary ignored him, energetically banging her one block on the table. He watched her, then took his blocks and put them away. Mary refused to surrender the one in her hand.

He took out some picture cards and showed them to her, asking her questions. She began to show interest. As she bent forward to get the picture cards I was able to retrieve the block she was holding.

'What's that?' he asked, pointing to a picture of a ball. Mary smiled at him, breathing a word even I couldn't understand. 'And this?' he asked. 'And this?' He showed her several cards, and asked her questions, related to a three-year-old's presumed interests. Instead of paying attention, she began to shift in the stroller, making dissatisfied noises. So he finally gave up and began making his notes.

Then Mary's face suddenly became bright red. Her body very stiff, she shot her legs straight out and clenched her fists. I wondered what had happened. Mark knew before I did. Sitting wide-eyed, he jabbed a finger in her direction, pinching his nose and rolling his eyes upwards. Soon Mary's face reverted to mere pink. She was finished with what she'd done, and what she'd done was now unmistakable. The smallness of the room helped trap the odour and the heat seemed to intensify it. By now Mark, his hand over his nose and mouth, was glaring at me as though I were the perpetrator. The psychologist pretended not to notice.

'Well,' he began, 'we have to assess her on the basis of what a three-year-old is normally able to do. Of course, Mary might be able to understand what to do, but be physically unable to do it. I mean she just hasn't had certain experiences. And so certain causal relations haven't dawned on her. She can't hold things very well. She had to use all her energy just to figure out how to pick something up, keep it in her hand, transfer it from one hand to another. Of course at this stage we're dealing only with the rudiments of intelligence.' He sounded anxious. 'I'm going to put Mary down as on the borderline between trainable and educable. But judging from the reports, and from what you say, she's not *merely* on the trainable level.'

'What does that mean, exactly?' As I asked the question, he must have groaned. The odour was ripening every minute. Patiently he launched into an explanation. 'On the lowest level, there is the person who is living pretty much as an infant. He eats and sleeps, and is completely dependent. He responds to love and attention as an infant would. He cries to get what he wants. There's not much, if any, speech.' He shook his head. 'Then there is the trainable person – who can be taught to take care of his or her own needs to some extent. To clothe himself, feed himself, toilet himself, take directions. Mary, I think, is capable of more than that. So we'll say she's beyond the trainable level, on the educable level – just barely. She'll go to school and learn how to count, learn the names of colours, learn the alphabet, learn songs.' He smiled again. 'But as you say, it's too soon to know for certain. As of now she tests out at about an eighteen-month level. We can be pretty sure she's educable. We don't *know*, but we have to make some judgement, inadequate as it may be. And that's it for the moment.' He stood up, gathered his sheets together and slid them into his folder. The psychologist waved at her and nodded to me. 'Bye-bye, Mary. Nice to see you.' I stood up and shook his hand, wanting to ask more questions, but knowing that Mary's condition brooked no further delay. Mark was up and pulling at the stroller, trying to angle it around so that he could swing it out the door. He pushed it and I carried Mary as we walked into the hall, dim now near the elevators.

'Let's get out of here,' Mark said. 'Gosh, Mary, what did you *do*?'

I changed Mary in the ladies' room, and we went out, got into the car and drove home. There Tom came out to meet us and brought Mary in. He lifted her against his chest. Pulling at his shirt, trying to hug him, she gave him her happiest smile.

'What did the psychologist say?' Tom asked as we walked indoors.

'Basically he didn't know. He agreed it was too soon to say. But he did make a guess: Her mental ability is that of an eighteen-months-old child.' There, I thought, I'd got it out quickly. Tom, who'd had such faith in her mental ability, didn't react. He sat down on the couch with Mary and wedged her between his legs in the kind of pretend standing position she liked. She moved her feet excitedly, a simulated walking. Her left foot kept crossing over her right, making it difficult for her to lift that foot at all. She didn't seem to mind. She kept exerting herself, putting great energy into the efforts.

'Eighteen months? And her actual age is three years, two months,' Tom said slowly.

'Yes. The psychologist gave her puzzles, blocks and picture cards. He asked her questions about herself. Her name, what she does every day – what you'd normally ask a child her age.'

'But she really hasn't had much of a chance to use puzzles and blocks. And her eyes aren't that good either,' Tom said as he stroked her hair.

'Yes,' I said.

'It's hard for her to hold things up to see them. She can't even sit by herself. And she can't just go and get things for herself. So she hasn't *done* a lot of the things a child of her age would have been doing for some time now. And without the experience, she doesn't have the concepts,' Tom concluded. 'I don't see how they can test her. It's not fair.'

'They have to do *something* – make some kind of guess.'

Tom shrugged. He didn't say anything more, and I went into the kitchen to start dinner. I was glad, in a way, that he was so determined to champion Mary's intelligence. But this conviction of his, that her mind had been left untouched by the brain damage, made me uneasy. Where would this position lead Tom, if Mary grew to be severely retarded? At first the gap wouldn't be so great, some of the experts said. But later on it would widen and become more obvious. Mental retardation would be much harder for Tom to accept than physical debility. He'd said so, often.

I peeled five potatoes. The smallest one had a gash at the end. I kept having to slice it deeper and deeper, until finally it was too small – a Mary potato. So I took another and started in again.

A Handicapped Child

In those days Mary's favourite recreation was crawling.
The living-room floor was carpeted, and we'd watch as she
pulled herself from one side of the room to another, rolling
under a table. Again and again she had to be discouraged
from trying to yank electrical cords from their sockets.
'God knows she's determined,' Tom used to say. Her
method for moving was to inch herself forward with her
elbows, her legs dragging behind her. Sometimes she'd
make futile efforts at a full crawl, hunching herself up on
her elbows, bringing her knees forward so she'd be
elevated. 'Look at you!' Mark would exclaim. 'You're
crawling just like a *person*!' And she'd smile, pleased and
excited, and go at it with a vengeance till, wobbling from
side to side, she'd finally topple over. If she managed to
progress at all when attempting a full crawl, it was by
accidentally falling forward while trying to prevent herself
from falling sideways. When she tumbled down, there'd be
a brief outburst of consternation, and she'd continue on in
pursuit of the goal she'd set herself. Sometimes it was to lift
the valance of the couch and wedge her body underneath,
trying to find what was hiding there in the darkness. Or
she'd make her slow way into the kitchen, go to the cabinet
doors, open each in succession, and then roll over and lie on
her back so that she could reach into the cabinet with her
right hand and lift out boxes or cans or bottles. Other times
she'd lie on her stomach, resting on her left elbow, her right
arm extended, her head raised so that she could see things
to take out. I'd marvel at her stamina, seeing her there on
her stomach, all her muscles straining, her open mouth

drawn down to one side, breathing heavily, lifting her head with an exhausting effort as high as she could lift it. When I'd pick her up she'd be filthy, her cheeks black, her hands grimy, dirt under her nails, bits of noodles, rice or cornflakes in her clothing. But she didn't give up. One way or another she always managed to get a lot of things down from the shelves.

One fall day while I was busy she managed to make her way from the living-room to the little terrace outdoors: we called it the patio. Though the two were on the same level, she'd had a wooden jamb and a screen door to contend with. On the terrace there was a tree, growing out of the cement, and around its trunk a tangle of vines and plants, and it was there I discovered her. The wind had carried dead leaves across the terrace and piled them there, along with feathers, dead insects and bits of paper. Mary, fascinated by the tangle around the base of the tree, was pulling at the vines, reaching and digging her fingers into the dirt and patting it. There she was: dry leaves and twigs in her hair, her shirt tugged up, her trousers down, one shoe off, resting her bare middle on the cold cement, in a drizzle of rain. I felt full of heartache, seeing her like that. *A handicapped child*. She can't do things other children can do. She can't stand up, she can't sit, she can't really crawl. Only twenty-five per cent of brain-damaged children escape retardation, I'd read. I saw how physically limited she was – how she rolled and dragged herself around. The sight of her there was disturbing. But then I thought: Why? She was very happy. She was doing exactly what she set out to do. I wondered: Would she ever know her limitations? I wondered whether, given all her handicaps, it wouldn't be a kind of blessing for her to be retarded.

While Mary was at home, I tried to work, usually in the office. The phone was there, and a typewriter stand and desk and work table. There were filing cabinets against the wall opposite, and boxes of files neatly stacked in a corner. When the door was closed it was a private cheerful place. Its high ceiling and two windows gave it an unwarranted feeling of spaciousness. I would type in there, and file papers and correspondence, and do my editorial chores – but only when Mary was occupied or sleeping. Once settled somewhere, she'd be content for half an hour at most; then she'd begin to fret and whimper. It was always a challenge to find something to entertain her. It was easier when the other children were home. Mark would take a blanket out to the lawn and the two of them would bounce around on it. Sometimes he'd make a tent and roll her in and out of it, or devise some kind of ball game for her. He'd push her in her stroller to the red wood bench on the terrace, and bring pans of water for her to float things in. He'd bring down her toys and surround her with them. Or he'd dance her dolls or his soldiers on the table animating them for her. He'd fix bread and butter for them, or he'd find a cache of contraband cookies and bring them out, whispering that she wasn't to tell. But after a half hour or an hour of invention he'd lose his enthusiasm. He'd become interested in his own ideas of play. 'Baby!' he'd say, which would make things worse. Then Mary would begin complaining about his inattention, and would fret or cry. After a stab at placating her, he'd come tell me he had some urgent mission. Off he'd go on his bike to see a friend. Mary would be in a worse state than ever, and all the toys and paraphernalia would have to be picked up and put away again.

Bonnie, too, had her other interests. All too soon she'd decide she was finished playing with Mary. She'd pick her up, sit her on the couch, and hug her. 'Bon-nie, Bon-nie,' Mary would sing, awkwardly clapping her hands. 'Got to go, Mom!' Bonnie would say, jumping up and leaping across the room. Suddenly she'd be out the door, waving both hands to Mary. 'Bye-bye, bye-bye,' she'd say, and name a friend she was going to visit. 'Be back in a while!' And Mary would cry, torrents of tears. So I'd have to stop working, pick her up, walk around the room with her or wander out into the kitchen to find something for her to do.

I must get some help, I kept saying. I wasn't getting my work done because of Mary – overseeing her, feeding her, exercising her, getting her down for her nap, getting her up; above all, entertaining her. I'd have to snatch at odd moments to do my work: artwork and editing, typing and filing. I'd been letting the housework slide till it became unmanageable. Sometimes I'd be near to tears, trying to type a letter. Sometimes a single letter would take two hours. I'd make elaborate schedules, but Mary's needs would throw them askew. For a while I thought I'd found a solution – to provide her with wastebaskets full of typing paper, odds and ends of junk mail envelopes, with coloured papers in them, spools of ribbon, and she'd amuse herself by transferring these to another basket. A variant of this was to hand over the little drawers of paper clips, erasers, staples, bottles of correction fluid, pencils, pens, index cards, scotch tape, rulers. She'd go through these, studying each thing carefully, putting it in a jiffy bag or container or box, fitting one thing in another and lifting it out again – an hour's worth of entertainment in this. And then there was the revolving tray. She'd take out all my brushes and pens, inspect all the bottles, taste the erasers, then try to put things in again. Or I'd let her start on the sewing box, taking out the spools of thread, spilling the safety pins into the tray, fitting the thimbles on her fingers or nose. But after a while she'd done all these tasks so often and at such length that she'd exhausted their satisfactions.

'Get me some junk, Mark,' I said one day. 'Lots of little things. Put them all in a box.' He scouted through the house and came up with assortments of small toys and kitchen utensils and junk jewellery – Mark knew what Mary liked. I got a lot of mileage out of his collections. Yet I was always buying time to work, it seemed, in the middle of the day I'd expend twice the energy and accomplish half of what I'd have in a normal office situation, and I'd be exhausted afterwards. Sometimes I found I couldn't even walk from one room into another, without picking her up and taking her with me. 'Mommy?' she'd plead. A pause and then the crying would start. She'll grow out of it, I kept saying to myself; this is only temporary. Bonnie and Mark, when younger, had demanded my time and attention. But Mary, I suspected, would always need someone to help her occupy her time. She'd never be able to go running off to visit friends, or disappear into the garden outside to build a fort or castle.

In the evening Mary was a pleasure: I no longer had the problem of trying to work and entertain her at the same time.

Tom had been encouraging me to get help. We had enough money to have someone in part time. I put an ad in one of the local papers. On Thursday, when the paper came out, the phone began to ring.

'How many hours?' a voice would ask.

'Four or five,' I'd say. 'It's flexible.'

'Three children, you say?'

'Yes. My youngest is handicapped. She's not sick or anything. She's just not able to get about herself. She needs help.'

'Oh? Handicapped.'

'The other two children pretty much take care of themselves. I need someone to take care of Mary, my youngest, and to fix dinner in the evenings for the three children. That's it, mostly.'

'Well, I don't think I'd be the one for that. Taking care of your handicapped child, I mean.'

'I see. Then you don't even want to come over to talk about it?'

'No. I'm sorry. But thanks, anyway.'

I'd made arrangements to see a candidate at three o'clock one day. She was seventeen, had a driver's licence, sounded confident and cheerful – just what I needed. Some time after three the phone rang.

'Mrs Collins?'

'Yes.'

'I'm very sorry. My daughter will have to cancel her appointment with you.'

'Oh? Is something wrong?'

'No. It's just that I've spoken to her. And I've taken her to see some children with cerebral palsy. She really had no idea what it was like. I don't want her to care for someone like that.' A pause. 'It's too much responsibility.'

'She sounded quite capable.'

'She is. But she's never been exposed to anything like that. And I think she's too young.'

'Well, thank you for calling.'

'Why didn't you mention Mary's handicap in the ad?' Tom asked that evening.

'Because, I guess, I didn't want to attract professional people. A practical nurse would be too expensive. And I'd rather have someone young.'

'Why don't you put another ad in, mentioning that Mary is handicapped. I'll help with the interviews.'

I tried that and the response was dramatic. For every call on the previous ad, there were three on this. Every caller was interested, and eager to find out more about Mary.

'My sister has CP,' one youngster said. Or there'd be a cousin or an uncle.

'This is weird,' I said to Tom, who joined me for the

interviews, 'So many people.'

He smiled, more than a little complacently.

In the end we chose a girl, Teresa, out of high school a year or so. She stayed with Mary during the day, bringing her out for errands and grocery shopping and trips to feed the ducks. She was soft-spoken and shy, but she was firm with Mary and had a good heart. When she finally had to move to New Mexico several months later, Mary had entered the preschool programme at St Charles.

The Clinic School

Mary didn't start the clinic school until November, after several months' delay to satisfy the bureacracies' appetite for paperwork. Her costs were funded under a combination of new government programmes for handicapped preschool children. On school days a bright yellow van arrived each morning at seven-thirty or so. I'd carry Mary out to the girl, a part-time college student who drove the bus. She'd scoop Mary up and strap her securely into an infant chair. Mary looked forward to leaving on the bus, and never cried on school mornings. In the afternoons she'd arrive home at 3.30, often dishevelled from the hour-long ride but usually beaming. She carried a yellow plastic lunch box; it had a strap she could hold on to and a zipper along the top for her to fiddle with. Inside would be little notes from the teacher, or a mimeographed sheet about a field trip which needed parental permission.

Bonnie and Mark would arrive home from school shortly before Mary, and there would be a hubbub of mingled voices with Mary's agitated cries or pealing laughter counterpointing the general chatter. She'd drink some milk and eat a snack, and I'd take her up to her crib where she'd lie down happily for her afternoon rest. She required certain bribes as the price of her co-operation. She'd be allowed to keep her shoes on, as a sign that she was not in bed for keeps but only for a rest. This understood, she had no objection to lying there and playing with her bunny or her dolls, or little Fisher-Price toys – on loan from Mark, who kept a sharp eye on them, enhancing their value. At five she'd be ready to come downstairs again, refreshed even if she hadn't slept, and would sit in her high chair (much later it was a specially built wheelchair) while I was fixing dinner, singing to herself or commenting on my activities. She'd become absorbed in any novelty placed on her tray – an egg beater, a muffin tin, measuring spoons. On some days nothing would satisfy her. Then I'd take her to the living-room, where she'd sit with Bonnie on one side and Mark on the other and they'd play with her and sing songs. Most of the time the two older children accepted her company unreservedly, with delighted and noisy acclaim for her achievements. When mere attention wasn't enough for her, one of the children would take her outside in the stroller. 'How long?' Mark would ask. 'Oh, just long enough to take her down the street and back,' I'd answer. Often they'd be back in no time at all, and she'd become my charge again. It took a long while, sometimes, to fix dinner.

Over the first few weeks we created a happy picture of Mary in school. It wasn't until a month later that we found out that her behaviour there had not been so wonderful as we'd supposed. At a meeting with her teacher and therapists one afternoon, I was shocked to learn that Mary, while at school, was constantly crying.

'Really?' I asked. 'She seems so happy: She loves getting on the bus. She comes home, most days, all smiles.'

The teacher rolled her eyes and gave me a lop-sided grin. The therapists laughed. Apparently I'd said something very funny.

'She's getting better, though,' said the physical therapist, a large, soft-spoken, thoughtful young woman with light blonde hair named Phyllis. Another, rather defiant woman shook her head energetically. 'No! You can't get Mary to do *anything* she doesn't want to do! Not Mary!'

'Oh,' I said. She'd cried a lot, I said, when she first went to the clinic in Ireland. I could see, I said, that that was hardly parallel – she wasn't even a year old then, and now she was more than three. 'What do you think, then?' I laughed half-heartedly. 'Is there any hope?'

'Oh, she'll get used to us,' said Phyllis. 'It'll take time. But really – she's already a little calmer.'

Mary, sitting there on my lap, refused to answer any questions. Nor would she go to anyone else.

'Mary,' Phyllis said. 'Come and show your mummy what kind of work we do.'

Mary, breathing faster, began to stiffen.

'Oh, come on, Mary,' I said, squeezing her. 'Show me what you and Phyllis do together!' Without further ceremony I handed her over to Phyllis, who sat down on an exercise mat with her legs extended and close together. She balanced Mary there, keeping her little legs apart and at right angles, and asked Mary to cross her right hand over, stretching it all the way down beyond her left knee to reach a rubber toy on the mat. At first Mary objected. But the girl held her firmly, coaxing and encouraging her. 'You can do it, Mary,' She said. 'I know you can. Stretch and stretch!' Mary, forcing herself to reach down, retrieved the squeaky toy. 'Good! Good!' said Phyllis, with genuine pride, and Mary gave a little snort of pleasure. The others in the room cheered her. 'Look at that!' her teacher said. 'We knew she could do it!'

'Keep it up, Mary,' Phyllis said.

Once again Mary leaned over, this time stretching her weaker left arm over to the right. This time she couldn't pick up the toy. But she'd tried hard, and they praised her, saying she'd do much better the next time.

'She *can* do it,' the girl insisted. 'Once she gets over the strangeness – '

At first dismayed at Mary's being balky and difficult, I felt a kind of pride in her effort here. 'And what should

Mary be doing at home, now?' I asked, filled with hope again. 'We've already been carrying her the way you've suggested – with her legs separated on either side of our waists – and we put her to bed on her side or on her stomach, and we try to make her sit forward, knees bent – '

'Keep doing that,' the young woman said earnestly. 'And when she sits be sure that she doesn't keep trying to thrust her head backward.'

I thought of her high chair, so big for her that she'd lean back in it like a stuffed doll, all one straight piece, her head touching the top of the backrest. 'When she eats, she has trouble sitting forward,' I said. 'At first she's fine, but then she begins to stiffen.'

To solve this problem and others like it, they began to discuss building fitted chairs for Mary. We'd get an insert that would make a snug fit for her high chair, forcing her to sit up, angling her knees and supporting the soles of her feet. The local carpenter, who did small jobs for the school, would devise a standing chair low enough to slide into the small tables at school so she could join the other children in their activities. And they'd order a wheelchair, especially adjusted for her.

'Do you have any other problems with Mary?' one of the therapists asked. 'Anything we might help with?'

'Well,' I said, 'the problem you have with her – the crying.'

At home, sometimes, Mary would be unable to explain what she wanted, or she'd be heartbroken at not being able to have or do something. So she'd work herself into an emotional state and not be able to shake it.

'Sometimes she has tantrums – crying jags,' I said.

'What do you do when either of the other children acts like that?' a dark-haired woman with glasses asked.

'They're sent to their rooms till they calm down,' I answered quickly. But I'd been tentative with Mary, I

193

said, reluctant to demand that she behave considerately, even more reluctant to punish her. I hadn't known whether she could understand why she was being punished. And it seemed harsh, to think of punishing a little one whose handicaps were so overwhelming.

'Do the same thing with Mary,' the woman said flatly. 'Whenever she cries like that, in anger or to get her own way, just take her to her room. Don't get angry yourself. Just be definite. When she stops crying, bring her back down again.'

This was a sensible thing to do, I realised. I left with Mary, shortly after that. These people were full of practical suggestions. Lifting her out of the stroller, I strapped her tightly into the car seat. It was easy for me to *imagine* handling Mary's crying jags, to *imagine* thinking up activities that would encourage Mary and inspire her . . . But the day-to-day drag of lifting and carrying, the quarter hours and half hours of purely physical care were beginning to drain my energy in a kind of steady seepage, and left me always a little empty.

For Mary the ophthamologist's office was a dark cave of wonders. There was a jiggling monkey which clanged cymbals together, a kind of movieola with an animated cartoon; lights of spectacular colours going on and off in different parts of the dark room. Mary was fascinated. While the doctor worked the gadgets, he peered into her eyes with a probe light.

'Your daughter,' he finally said, 'is a juvenile myope.'

I knew that she'd have great difficulty reading because of her poor eyesight. No *Sesame Street* for a little girl who could hardly distinguish figures on a television screen.

He finished his tests. From his answers to my questions, I learned what I'd already half-known, that Mary's vision was so limited, that without glasses she'd be considered legally blind. My comments assumed, naturally, that her intelligence would be affected.

He shook his head, saying in a matter of fact tone, 'Oh, no, Mrs Collins, she's a lot brighter than anyone realises.'

When the tests were over, Mary demanded to be let down on to the floor, 'Bye-bye,' she kept saying, moving towards the door with her awkward hitching movement. I scooped her up and carried her out into the anteroom. The doctor's patients watched while we waited to receive the doctor's written prescription for lenses, and listened to Mary's fretful impatient requests to be let down on to the floor again. When I had the prescription in hand, she turned to the people in the waiting-room. 'Go bye-bye in the car!' she loudly announced.

A few weeks later she got the glasses, and to our surprise consented to leave them on. Wearing the thick lenses gave her a comical aspect, making her look like a little scholar.

One day in December I realised that something had happened to me.

It was a cold morning. Mary had already gone off in her little yellow school bus. Through the kitchen window I watched Bonnie and Mark trudging across the frost-packed grass, through the loose dead leaves, towards the bus stop a block away. I saw them disappear into the street, beyond bare grey trees that stretched into a greyer sky. I collected the waste baskets and, opening the back door, carried them out to the trash cans. The day was dry and still and so cold it hurt to breathe deeply outdoors. I hurried back. The warmth and quiet in the house seemed to wrap me around. When I'd distributed the empty baskets, I went to the window of the living-room. Everything seemed so peaceful, so tranquil. The dullness of the sky made the world seem a monochrome quilt – grey trees, grey grass, grey terrace stone. The slabs of the sky coloured even the interior, laying a glaze of grey over the blue rug, the red brick fireplace, the soft pine boards panelling the walls. And I recalled just then what an art teacher of mine in college had always said. 'Keep your palette simple. You'll be surprised at the nuances you can get. And *then* – when you put in a bright colour!' His face would light up with an ecstatic smile, and he'd gesture as though adding a final stroke of his brush: '*See how it sings!*'

I looked around the room. There was no brilliant spot of red singing out: there was only a pillow quietly radiating its turquoise from the couch, and the cat curled up beside it. I felt a surging, piercing joy, and that tranquil even-toned dullness that wrapped the room into the grey cold winter outdoors made my joy all the more glorious.

And suddenly I knew why I was so happy. The screaming inside me had, once and for all, gone away. I knew I'd crossed a divide and would never feel that terrible sensation ever again. It had disintegrated. It was now nothing. There would only be the memory of it, as one is tender about the place where a physical pain was once felt.

Hydrocephalus

Every month there was a cerebral palsy clinic at St Charles, a kind of seminar where the parents would meet with the doctors and therapists on each child's team to discuss the child's progress. The emphasis at the earliest meetings was on Mary's lack of muscle control. We discussed her problems of rolling over, her patterns of crawling, her lack of head and trunk control, her difficulties in sitting up and holding things, her poor vision.

As I came home after one of these sessions, I found that something was troubling me – I'd been neglecting to ask them about the size of Mary's head. Not that it was grossly or unpleasantly disproportionate; it just didn't seem that it should be so large. 'She looks like one of those kids in the Campbell's Soup ads,' Bonnie had once said. Yes! Mary had the same pretty round face, the short curly hair and chubby cheeks, the wide-apart big eyes, the small pert mouth – all set in an exaggeratedly large head on a tiny body.

'Maybe it's just that her arms and legs are so thin,' Tom said. 'She's *always* looked like that,' was Mark's comment. True, her head had always seemed overlarge. I thought of my disquiet when visiting Mary at The Cottage Home – Ann Burrows holding Mary in her arms, in the dark hallway, the light behind them and the glancing notion that there were two adult heads – that Mary's head seemed almost as large as Ann's. With so much else to think about, I hadn't paid more attention, and I'd been confident then and since that the specialists would catch and attend to anything problematic. At St Charles Mary had been under daily scrutiny by people who knew far more than I about cerebral palsy. But I decided to raise the question on my next visit to the clinic.

The paediatrician was a soft-spoken Indian woman with a dot on her forehead and a sari beneath her white doctor's jacket.

'I think Mary's head is too large,' I said.

'When did you begin to think so?' she asked.

'First, when I visited her in Ireland, after I hadn't seen her for over a year.'

'How old was she then?'

'Two.'

'And do you think it is larger now than it was then?'

'No. But the proportion between her head and body – it still isn't right.'

'Is she irritable?'

'Not usually. Happy and cheerful most of the time.'

'Is she often listless?'

'No. Not really. Only sometimes, when she just sits there, tuning everything out. Do you think there's anything wrong?'

'Well, I don't know. Perhaps she had a condition which has now been arrested. We will measure her head.' She did this with a centimetre tape and wrote down the number on a sheet.

'Are there head measurements in the records from Ireland?' I asked.

'No. I don't have any in the folder here. Nothing I can compare. I will measure her again before the clinic meets each month. And you should watch to see if she shows any special signs of irritability – if she becomes unusually cranky and tired, or begins to be nauseous.'

As a high school freshman I'd worked as an aide in a hospital ward. I'd seen Philip the Waterhead Baby – a year-old boy. He had not been expected to live long, but he continued to lie there for months, crying listlessly, unable to close his eyes because the skull had so expanded and stretched the skin that his eyelids were useless.

I was worried. And so during the next several months I pursued this question. Finally, in late spring, the paediatrician agreed to arrange for an examination by the neurosurgeon.

'Mrs Collins is concerned about the size of her daughter's head,' the paediatrician said in a doubtful voice. 'She feels it may be too large.' Mary was sitting up on the examining table.

'Of *course* it's too large!' he said. 'Just looking at her you can tell her head's not a normal size!' He held Mary's head in his hands. 'Unless she's a monster,' he added abruptly, looking neither at the paediatrician nor at me. 'She'll need a brain scan to discover whether the ventricles are enlarged. I'll see her again after I look at the pictures.' He told the paediatrician to arrange to have me take Mary to a hospital not far away, which had one of the new machines for computerised axial topography – a CAT scan, as it was called.

'What will he do if the scan shows the ventricles are enlarged?' I asked the paediatrician afterwards. 'He will put a shunt in her head,' Her Indian accent played havoc with the vowels: 'He weel poot a schant in hair hed.' The shunt, she explained, would draw off fluid from the brain cavity. She tapped Mary's skull, above the right ear. A thin tube goes into the brain area. A valve goes in here at the side of her head. It feels like a button. The tube is extended under the skin down along her neck and into her chest and then into her abdomen. The tube carries away the excess fluid from the brain. It is eventually absorbed in her abdominal cavity.' I'd never heard of such a bizarre procedure.

'This shunt – is it something new?'

'Oh, no. Not really. Usually, if there's some indication of hydrocephalus, it's done shortly after birth. It's a common operation.'

'Does the shunt hurt?'

'No, no. They can't even feel it. There's a small scar and then the hair grows over it. You can't see it. When you put your hand on the head, you can feel the button – that's the valve – which is there so that you can make sure the shunt is working, that there's no blockage. If there's blockage, you clear the shunt by pressing the button. You can feel it go in and then pop out again.'

'And if the shunt weren't put in?'

'Well, the pressure of the fluid might damage the brain cells eventually – '

It disturbed me that the problem had not been diagnosed before this. I resolved, though, to put the past out of my mind. What had happened, had happened.

A few weeks later Mary was given the CAT scan. Soon after I saw the neurophysician again. His time was tightly scheduled. He had private appointments in his own office elsewhere. At the hospital I waited with a group of parents gathered in an anteroom. The pictures – brain scans of our children – would be brought to him when he emerged from his surgery. He'd talk to each parent while re-examining each child.

It was a long wait. He came out and summoned one set of parents. Another couple, waiting next to me, began talking about him. 'He's fantastic,' the woman said. 'He's done a lot for so many kids.' Her husband looked at her, stubbing his cigarette into the standing tray, 'No bedside manner,' the husband said. 'He don't care what he says or who he says it to. He's okay, though. He tries. A lot of them doctors don't like to work on these kids unless it's going to make 'em *all* better. They don't see the point. Think it's not worth their time.'

'What do you mean?' I asked.

'You hear stories. Some of them, if a kid is really bad, you know, and he'll never be much of anything – some of them doctors – they say, don't bother with him, let him alone.'

I wondered whether he was making that up. Probably not. It was an American enough assumption, and hadn't I shared it? As much as anyone, I was a consumer of the American dream. I'd woven its pretty colours into the fabric of my own thinking. I'd had no preparation for a child like Mary. I'd assumed that my children would exhibit all the special signs – the sunshine wholeness, the starlight gifts. They would fling themselves across green fields on storybook afternoons. The future for my children would lie before them like a new dawn of the world. Other people's children might be broken before the game was started, or fallen and damaged along the dark wayside. But never ours. We would never have to spend our high energies lifting little ones whom life's river had left, damaged goods, on the dock.

'Yes,' the neurosurgeon said when my turn finally came. He took some large grey photographic sheets out of an orange folder – Mary's CAT-scan prints. 'The ventricles are far too large. You can see it if you just look at these prints – there, and there, and there.'

Your Heart Goes Out

'When you've brushed your teeth,' I said, 'give me a hoot and I'll come up and kiss you good-night.'

'Okay,' Mark said. But his mind was far, far away.

Tom and I were sitting on the couch, he in his corner near the bookcase, his pencils, books, dictionaries and atlas, all his paraphernalia, arranged there on the shelves and coffee table. Mark, his face ruddy from his bath, wore his red and blue striped pyjamas, bottoms pulled high on his chest and top unbuttoned and askew. Absently he wandered over to Tom. Then suddenly he seemed to know where he was. His face broke into a great smile. 'Night, Daddy!' he said. Swooping down, planting a kiss on Tom's face, he spun around and did a little jig, a kind of Charlie Chaplin number, hopping on one foot and then the other, his arms flailing about.

'What's that for?' Tom asked, with an amused smile.

'I don't know,' said Mark, using his little boy voice, rolling his eyes. Then he stopped suddenly, looking shy and foolish.

'Goodnight, then!' Tom laughed. Reaching out, he took a striped arm and drew Mark over and hugged him.

Mark blushed and smiled. With another little hop, he ran from the room and went pounding up the stairs, where he discovered the cat. I heard her take the sharp turn at the top of the stairs, heard her claws skitching in the upper hallway, and imagined her zooming in a full arc into the farthest bedroom. I knew she'd made her escape when I heard the bathroom door close, and the sound of water running. Tom, his grey hair shining in the island of light from the lamp, put down his book. 'There's no such thing,' he said slowly, 'as loving one child more than another. It's not possible.' He seemed surprised at what he was saying.

'You love each the same?'

'More than that, Pat.' He laughed as though he'd been tricked into admitting it: 'Your heart goes out completely to each one.'

'Hooo, hoot!' came the owl-like sound from Mark upstairs. Tom had crossed his legs and was settling himself in with his book. I knew what he meant, and I thought about it as I began to climb the steep stairs. I heard Mark tumbling into bed. I found him with the covers floating all over – his slapdash bedmaking. He was struggling to arrange matters so that his face would be on the pillow and the covers up to his chin. He closed his eyes, his mouth primly pursed for a kiss. Then I went to say goodnight to Bonnie.

'Does Mary have to be operated on?' she asked faintly.

'Yes, she does. It will help her.'

'How's Mary now?'

'Fine. She's fast alseep, I think.'

'And Mommy?'

'Yes?'

'Jane's fine, too.'

'Jane?'

'My hamster.'

'Oh, that's good.' Today, Jane, Tarzan's widow (the cat had finally got to Tarzan) had been inundated by a flood in her cage caused by a faulty water bottle. This afternoon I'd found Bonnie in the upstairs bathroom solicitously blow-drying Jane, as the hamster circled frantically around the sink, her fur riffled by the hot jet flow from the machine in Bonnie's hand.

'I'm glad she's fine,' I said, as I kissed Bonnie good-night. Next I went to the small bedroom to check up on

Mary. She was in her crib in the far corner. With the moonlight coming in the window, I could see her clearly. She was sleeping as she always slept, jacknifed on her side, with one hand free to clutch the slat of the siderail, but what I was thinking was how she looked when she was awake, how the thick lenses mounted on her tiny nose made her eyes seem smaller, how she followed everything, studied everything – so eager to please, to co-operate, to accommodate. How hard she had to try to achieve even little things! 'I can do it all by myself,' was Mary's refrain. Her bottom resting against the couch, she would vainly try to pull herself, half-sitting, half-standing, to the coffee table. Or she would try to sit forward on the green chair, grasping the armrest with her right hand, waving her left hand in the air as if for ballast as she swayed precariously. I pulled the cover up over her thin little shoulders, leaving her arm free to reach out to the rail. That was what Tom meant! It was their reaching out – their striving, despite all the evidence – overwhelming to us, the parents – of their littleness, their incapacity, their dependency. They reached out anyway – shakily, ineptly, foolishly, trustingly: blindly trying even to console and comfort us. *Your heart goes out completely to each one.*

As I turned away from Mary I heard something thumping in the closet, and out stepped Priscilla the cat, grandly unconcerned. I could see only her white muzzle and white paws advancing, supporting a shadow which brushed against me. Tail high, as she sidled along, she sashayed slowly to the door. Shadowy questions hung about as she disappeared into the lit hallway. I left the room, turned off the hall light and started downstairs. 'Could you leave it on, Mom?' Mark's voice, pretending to be anxious. 'I need it on.' So I flicked the switch.

What about Mary's future? A lurking thought, a hackle, a point of friction, a stumbling block – and I recoiled whenever my mind rubbed against it. It was like a jagged edge, ripping at the tidy seams of my thinking. If God were a human father, wouldn't He love the black Pentecostal babies up on One Hundred Sixth Street as wholeheartedly as He loved the white Episcopalian babies in their Crisscraft carriages on Sutton Place? And He'd love Mary, wouldn't He, as much as He loved Bonnie and Mark?

There was only silence in the hall as I continued slowly down the stairs.

An Operation

The operation was scheduled for early morning. At nine the neurosurgeon called to say that it had been successful. 'She'll be under the anaesthetic for several hours. She seems fine.' He'd completed his work. The shunt had been implanted in little Mary's skull.

'Thank you,' I said.

'Good. That's all, Mrs Collins.'

At first I was going to delay a day in going to see her. What good would it do to go right away? She wouldn't quite understand; I might upset her. She'd think I'd come to take her home, and she'd be heartbroken when I'd have to leave. Or maybe she wouldn't wake at all. And what would be the good then in a round trip drive of two and a half hours?

I decided to call the hospital.

'She's stirring.' The nurse spoke in a cheerful sing-song. 'She's awake – '

'Do you think I should come?'

'It's entirely up to you, Mrs Collins.' Sing-song.

'I see,' I said quickly. 'I'll be there before four.'

'Can I come?' Bonnie launched into her pleading act, jumping up and down. 'Please. Oh, please!'

'She won't even be awake, and they might not let you see her at all.'

'That's okay. I don't care. Just let me come. I just want to see Mary. See what the place is like?'

'All right. We'll bring her night clothes,' I said, 'and her glasses.'

'Oh, gosh, yes! Mary won't like being in that bed

without her glasses on. And I'll get her shoes and socks.' She raced up the stairs. I could hear her busily opening drawers.

She came down soon with a packed black duffel bag, and Mary's furry rabbit. 'All set,' she said breathlessly. 'I packed a few other things I thought Mary would want.' I looked into the bag – a nightgown, underclothes, shoes, socks, skirts, jeans, sweaters, sweatshirts, and a tin of band-aids.

'So I see,' I said.

It was one of the dog days, during the time of the ascendancy of the dog star, a period of prolonged hot sticky weather. The car's air conditioning wasn't working and our clothes were sticky. St Charles was on the north shore, which was always more humid. There was no breeze, just the hanging hot muggy air. As we left the car, Bonnie, her skin glistening with perspiration, dragged the bag out of the back seat. 'Mary's not going to need any sweaters!' she said.

No one was at the attendant's booth in the lobby.

'We'll just go up,' I said. 'We won't wait to ask if you can come with me. We're just bringing clothes, you know.' We knew there was some prohibition about children under twelve visiting the wards.

'Oh, yes!' Bonnie's eyes gleamed. We walked to the bank of elevators.

The doors opened on to the second floor. There were murals, a Mickey Mouse and a Donald Duck, on the white walls. 'This is it,' Bonnie stage-whispered, hurrying out of the elevator. She looked half-triumphant, half-frightened – fearing, perhaps, what she might see in a hospital. Several small wheelchairs were lined up along the ward hallway. I could hear children crying. A chubby little girl in a bathrobe swung around the corner on crutches.

'Wait here,' I said. Bonnie looked crestfallen. 'Don't

worry,' I said. 'I'll find out whether you can see Mary.' She seated herself in one of the chairs, looking at the child on crutches. I hurried down the hallway.

'Mrs Collins?' The duty nurse rose and smiled. 'We have Mary here in the room right across the hall, so that we can keep an eye on her. She's fine. Not quite awake yet, though.' In the darkened room opposite the desk, Mary was in a crib bed, an intravenous bottle hanging from a stand beside her. In the big crib she looked very tiny. A tautly stretched white sheet tucked over her chest, she lay on her side, her right arm limp above the sheet, her left arm attached to the plastic IV tube. In her nose was another tube, which fed over the side of the mattress to a jar on the lower shelf of the bedside table. The hospital gown swam up around her, its frayed cotton ends tied in big bows at the back. She lay, without a pillow, flat on the mattress. A large white bandage covered the right side of her head; her neck seemed far too tiny to support it. Her face was white, her mouth faintly open. Her eyes were shut, dark lashes resting on pale sheeks. She didn't respond when the nurse called her name.

'You said she's fine –'

'Oh, the operation went very well. She was vomiting earlier, so we put the stomach tube in. There's a little blood there, from the shunt drain in her abdomen; it probably bumped into something inside. Nothing to worry about, but we're keeping an eye on it.'

'Oh.' Beside the pain of the skull opening, the two trunk incisions, and the nausea, she had the stomach tube – I felt awed at what this little body could endure.

'Your mommy's here,' the nurse repeated.

'Mary,' I whispered. 'Mary, can you hear me?'

'I'll be at the desk if you need me,' said the nurse.

'Mary,' I whispered again.

I saw her move convulsively, her chest heaving, her eyes

opening, her hands tightening into tiny fists, her mouth quivering as she tried to speak. There were little explosions of air, then the words, 'Mommy, oh, Mommy!' It seemed that she wanted to cry but wasn't able to.

'Yes, honey. I'm here. You're a good girl, Mary. Such a good, good girl.'

'Mommy,' she repeated. Her mouth, closed tight, stretched down at the corners, her chin trembling. I wanted to pick her up and hug her. I searched for something to say.

'You'll have a good sleep, honey. You'll feel better. I love you, we all love you, Mary. You'll be all right – all better. You'll be fine.' I began to rub her back. 'And Bonnie's here too,' I whispered.

'Bonnie? Bonnie – ' she said with effort.

'When I come back again, I'll bring Bonnie in here to see you. Will that be all right? You have a nice sleep and tomorrow we'll be back.' I didn't want her to think she could come home again now. If I let her think that, she'd be more upset and confused. I felt so heartless. But for the next few minutes she seemed content to have me rub her back. Seeing her fingers curl and uncurl I knew she was still half awake. Her lips were dry, and she was moving her tongue on them restlessly.

'Water,' she murmured.

'Yes, I'll get the nurse, honey.' I turned from the bed, walked out into the brightness of the hall, and asked the nurse to give Mary some water. 'She seems so thirsty,' I said.

She glanced at the clock. 'Yes. We'll give her a little bit at five. Don't worry.' She looked down the hall and saw Bonnie anxiously standing there, holding the black bag.

'That's my older daughter,' I said. 'She hoped to be allowed to see Mary. And we brought some things.'

'Oh, bring her over. Sometimes the children cause

problems, you know. That's why we have the rule. But we make our own judgements, really.' She waved at Bonnie, who bounded up the hall. Solemn and wide-eyed, she followed us into the room, and stood at the bed nervously, staring at Mary. 'Hi, Mary,' she said. 'It's Bonnie! I came to see you. Mary?'

Mary squirmed, again trying to speak but unable to. Finally she managed to say Bonnie's name.

'I brought your nightgown – ' Bonnie announced shyly. She moved closer to display the bag. 'And your bunny, too.' In the half-light of the hospital room I could see, Bonnie's eyes were filling.

'Mary's fine,' I said to Bonnie. I turned to rub Mary's back again. 'You'll feel better, Mary, when you sleep some more ' I bent down. 'You're a good girl,' I whispered in her ear. 'A great girl. A grand great girl!' I meant it. I felt humbled in the presence of this tiny pain-filled person. 'Tomorrow, honey, we'll be back.'

Her chin trembled and she struggled to open her eyes, but they slid around as she tried to focus them. As she strained to see my face I kissed her and forced a grin. Then Bonnie leaned over and kissed her on the head. We both turned and walked quickly away.

In the hallway, Bonnie struggled to keep back tears, rubbing her eyes with her fists. What could I do to lessen Mary's suffering and pain? What could I do to make it up to her? We stepped into the elevator and the doors whirred shut.

'Can I come with you tomorrow?'

'Yes, Bonnie. We'll come every day.'

I kicked at the starter of the car. Why does Mary have to suffer so much? I asked myself. Why can't she see well? Why can't she walk – or even sit up? Why all this fluid pressing on her brain? Why do her legs scissor? I felt an anger at the pain closing in around her tiny innocence.

Each day I went to the hospital. I stood at the long window in the hallway quietly watching her for a few minutes before letting her know we'd arrived. The fourth day I was alone, and lingered there at the window. This time Mary was propped up in a wheelchair. The bandage still covered the right side of her head. Her glasses looked a little cock-eyed from the bulk over her ear. In the bed, her head and shoulders propped up now by a big pillow, she always wore her glasses, and she was wearing them in the wheelchair, a wheelchair far too big for her and stained and battered with age and use. She was fully clothed, a belt fastened tight around her middle, her arms gripping the armrests as she surveyed the ward. On wheels next to her was a tall pole support, from which dangled a bottle of intravenous fluid, the tube looping down into a needle secured with a wide bandage on her thin little arm. On her feet she wore her black patent leather straps, her 'party shoes'. How small she looked, sitting there, and yet how regal! I felt pity, I felt admiration, thinking of all she had suffered and had still to suffer. I kept staring at her, the white face, the bluish rings around her eyes, her tiny tense fingers, her small figure parked alongside the large white metal crib, monumental in its solidity.

I saw her fragility confirmed, as when one holds one's hand up to the light to cut off the bright beams but instead they filter through. I saw her helplessness, saw that there was no reason that she exist. She could have vanished away, as I, to my shame had once wanted her to. I was looking at an apocalyptic little girl, in whom the struggle between good and evil, and the mystery of pain, suffering and diminishment were manifest. But I had to cheer – for her glowing face, so intent and serious as she gazed around her; for her efforts to reach out, to marshal her tiny energies. When Mary spoke her entire body spoke, her whole energy summoned into the labour of speaking –

muscles tensing, arms crooked, knees unflexed, legs suddenly rigid and straightening, her breath coming hard to form words in the air she expelled. Sometimes she couldn't complete the words, and had to squeeze herself to force out the last bit of air, her chin dropping and her arms tight to her chest, her little fingers fisting up or fanning out with her exertions. To speak at all she had to summon all her resources; to do this she had to make her whole organism suffer. I saw her eyes search the room, peering out over the glasses perched on the tip of her nose, one eye wandering a little to the side as she moved her head to try to focus on the clues she was following. Mary, I silently cried out, how could I have been so blind?

I went into the room, following a nurse who was bringing in a tray of food from the big wheeled cart in the hallway. The nurse deftly set Mary's tray on its stand, then whirled away towards the doorway.

'Mary!' I said.

Mary started, then reached out her arms.

'This – is my – muvver,' Mary said to the nurse, in a breathless, deliberate voice. 'How do you do?' the nurse asked me, with mock formality. Mary beamed. 'Sit down,' she said, anxious that I might suddenly disappear. I helped her with her lunch. Mary's appetite was good. It was a small enough appetite at best, but its return meant she was recovering. 'I want bread and butter,' Mary said, 'and potatoes!' She was happy now, and full of small eager chatter.

Each day we came to visit, we saw her improve. She'd accepted being in the hospital. She didn't need the IV any more. The nurses and aides were kind to her and Mary took a new interest in everything around her. Sometimes another child would be pushing her wheelchair, making circles around the room, or wheel her into the hallway for a trip up and down. With happy smile and alert face, her hands gripping the wheelchair's high sides, she'd grandly survey the passing scene. A nurse would drop by every few minutes to check. Other children would come over to Mary and offer to get a toy for her. 'That one,' she'd say, waving her arm in an arc towards a collection of toys. A child would bring the one he thought Mary wanted, and sometimes she'd smile and accept it. Sometimes she'd shrink back. 'No, no,' she'd say, her mouth quivering at the corners. Then an older child would come and bend over her and ask what was the matter. Again Mary would try, but be unable to steady her arm enough to point out the toy. She'd start in on the tears, but she'd want to be thought of as a big girl and a good girl, so she'd willingly accept some other toy.

After she'd stayed a full three weeks in the hospital, I came one day, Bonnie and Mark with me, to take her home. Two nurses accompanied us to the front door. I got the car, and circled around to the front door. Sitting there, her bandages off, Mary looked thin and pale. Her eyes were sparkling. But the right side of her head looked strange, the black stitches standing out over the pinched fold of skin on her scalp, over which a dusting of light brown hair had begun to grow. I wondered what effect the shunt operation would have on her. The doctor had said it would be perhaps three months before there would be any noticeable improvements, and he didn't think that then it would be anything dramatic. He hoped, he said, that the shunt would at least prevent further paralysis. But somehow I was beginning not to care whether she would improve. I was beginning to be willing to take her exactly as she was, even if she could never sit up, never say much, never progress in intelligence. She'd still be precious. She was so loving, so giving – and she'd suffered so much. As she sat there, she lurched forward, gathering herself into an announcement: 'We go back' – she had to pause to gulp some more air – 'home now.' She seemed to feel that by stating it she could magically ensure it.

'Off we go,' I said. 'To Mary's house.'

'Yes, yes!' she squealed, her arms and legs waving in excitement.

More pain

There is a long straight street in the town where we lived
then, a tree-lined, beautiful lane with grassy mounds on
either side and no sidewalks. In the summer, when the full
trees overhang the street, there is a tunnel-like effect and,
as one looks all the way down, the edges of the street seem
to converge at a point where the dappled grey road seems
to vanish into the greenness gathering in the distance.
Driving down this street one day, preparing to make my
usual left turn, I saw something sitting there, to the right,
way down beyond the intersection where I'd be turning
off. *Something:* I could find no name for it. I only knew it was
bright blue, standing in a patch of bright sunlight. What
on earth? I could find no meaning or purpose for it, no
reason for its being there. Hunched over the wheel, I kept
staring at the thing. I felt giddy; it kept resisting me,
remaining alien. And yet it was there, bright blue, curved,
brilliant against the tunnel of shade – an audacious,
bold, rude, impertinent, gaudy thing. I was awestruck.
Squinting ahead, I moved very slowly into the turn. As I
crossed the road, I suddenly saw it for what it was – the old
odd job truck I'd often seen around town, with makeshift
board sides in the back above the shallow loading bed,
with a vintage narrow and curved cab. It was painted a
swimming-pool blue, very unusual for a truck. So I'd
satisfied my curiosity, and calmed odd fears; yet I had the
strangest feeling of disappointment. Travelling down the
street, I'd been in awe of it. I'd felt myself in the presence of
some mysterious and even frightening thing, belonging to
some realm of being beyond the reach of my equations.

And I would see it afterwards, that bright blue thing of vision, and I can see it now – big, bold, gaudy, strange, abnormal, audacious, beautiful, of no apparent use, yet somehow very precious.

Like Mary, I kept thinking afterwards. The blue thing, while still a thing of vision, was like Mary! *Like Mary* – a puzzle, a conundrum that somehow revealed an exalted answer and an exalted question both at once. And it occurred to me that I had a lot to learn from the riddling in old folk tales. The simpleton, going off to seek his fortune, is confronted by a barrier which he cannot pass unless he answers a very odd question or complies with a weird request. And the simple-minded hero does what he is asked, though he doesn't know why. Everyone laughs at him, but it always turns out that by his innocent, obedient act he has unlocked some mystery at the same time as he gained a prize beyond his dreams.

'What use,' Ben Franklin asked, 'is a new-born baby?' What use is an abnormal child, an abnormal adult? What use to society a little girl who can't stand on her own two feet? Well I couldn't say, really. I didn't know. But I began to understand that such difficulties were irrelevant, at least in the terms in which they were likely to be stated.

Five weeks later, during the first week of September, I had to take Mary back to the hospital again, this time because the tendons controlling her leg muscles were too tight. They caused her legs to scissor when she extended them, and this scissoring was pulling her left leg bone out of its hip socket. So the tendons had to be cut. This meant another, and a far more painful, operation.

Once again I took her to St Charles Hospital. Once again the elevator doors opened on to Mickey Mouse and Donald Duck. I felt Mary's little body go stiff with tension.

Her fists clutching my neckline, she clung to me and wailed. 'I'm going home!' she cried, her voice high and tremulous. Then, uncertain of what was happening, she tried to force a cheerful laugh. 'I'm going with you! Amn't I, Mommy?' There was another sad little laugh. She was trying desperately to maintain hope that this was merely a visit and not a stay.

'Yes, honey. After a few days.'

Hearing her worst fears confirmed, Mary caved into me, pressing her face against my neck and uttering long, chest-filling cries. As we came to the nurses' station, she was trembling and trying to hide her face. Moving her knees frantically she half-crawled up my chest. She cried and cried, and not till half an hour later did she stop. By then her face was red and puffy, her hair in damp ringlets except for the right side of her head where the scar from the shunt showed beneath a light growth of hair. She drank some milk and ate a few bites of supper from a tray. Afterwards she let me give her a bath – a pre-surgical antiseptic had been added – in the adjoining tub room. When I left she was sitting in a wheelchair, dressed in her nightgown but with her shoes and socks on and wearing her glasses. A nurse went with Mary and me to the elevator, and took the wheelchair as I stepped in through the open doors. Looking stricken again, Mary burst into tears. As the doors closed I saw her legs stiffen, saw her reach out to me helplessly. I tried to stuff my unruly feelings away. I was wild with remorse. I struck my fist against the elevator door. I just managed to compose myself as I reached the lobby level. I walked miserably past the desk through the door and out into the muggy night.

This time Mary's recovery was far more difficult than after the shunt operation. Every movement of her trunk or legs caused her pain. Her legs had to be kept apart so that the muscles would lengthen and their tension would no longer work to pull her leg bone from its hip socket. So she was confined to the crib bed, her legs tied to the railings on either side. She was wan, restless and terribly distraught. She suffered for days and days. Finally she recovered enough to be able to sit in a wheelchair. As the pain receded, she began to recover her good spirits. She became interested in the other children of the ward, in the activity of the nurses.

Bonnie, Mark and I made the two-and-a-half-hour round trip a daily commute. Mary was a bright child now, alert and full of curiosity. When we arrived, we'd watch her at first from a distance playing with other children – laughing, singing; a willing passenger in the wheelchair on long journeys up and down the hall. Sometimes she'd be bumped into other children by a pusher too small to see where he was going, and she'd find this hilariously funny. Other times she'd accompany a nurse making rounds from room to room on the ward. Mary would sit there, her glasses on, her head tilted to the left, a frown of absorption on her face; suddenly the nurse would say some teasing or cheerful thing to her, and she'd break into her wide sweet smile.

Sitting with Mary one day in an elevator alcove, I was leafing through the magazines on the table, when a heavy figure emerged from the hallway, weaving slightly – probably, I thought, a father of one of the children. He staggered as he reached the elevator. Seeing us, he forced a smile. Ignoring the elevator button, he advanced towards me.

'I know Mary,' he said, his voice slurring. 'Hi, Mary. And hello, Mary's mother! That's who you are, isn't it?' He reeked of gin and all his gestures were exaggerated. 'Mary's mother? I mean –' He wore a white shirt, open at the neck, the sleeves rolled half-way up. On his forearms were elaborate blue tattoos: coiling snakes, anchors, other intertwined symbols – a Popeye figure, with dark blue trousers and heavy shoes. 'My son's here,' he said apologetically. He gave a boy's name – a German name. Suddenly he began to cry. He squinched his eyes shut. His mouth, which had been almost closed, stretched wide and he began making wheezing sounds: 'Hee, hee, hee, hee.'

'I'm sorry,' I said. He was swaying towards us. Mary looked startled.

'I try to be a good father. I do – oh, God, I do.' He shook his head violently, nearly losing his balance.

'I know,' I said. Somehow I knew that he *did* try, and that in his own estimation he had already failed: despair, with tattooed arms.

'Thank you,' he wheezed. 'Thank you. God bless you. You *do* know. I know, too.' He struggled to lift his head up, fighting back tears. But his self-pity kept bending him forward. He tried to stifle racking sobs, waving his hands as if he wanted to erase his own presence. He turned and disappeared around the corner back into the hallway, only to emerge a few seconds later, a nurse leading him by the elbow.

'Tomorrow,' she said, pushing the button. The doors opened. 'Good-bye,' she said cheerfully, as she guided him into a car. He waved to us, and the doors closed. The nurse whirled away, winking at us and shaking her head as she passed.

I gave her an uncomfortable half-smile.

Two and a half weeks later Mary came home again, still in pain from the incisions in her groin and the cut tendons. The raw openings at the junction of her trunk and legs were slow to heal.

A Flowering

It would take at least three months, the neurosurgeon had said, before we'd even begin to be able to assess the effectiveness of the shunt. It took some time after the second operation on her tendons before she could return to the clinic school with its day-to-day demands. I had plenty of time to wonder what good, after all, the shunt operation had done her. So far Mary couldn't sit up any better than before. So far there was no physical benefit. Had the second operation been a setback, somehow preventing the shunt from improving her condition? Still the shunt had to be a good thing, didn't it, draining excess fluid so that her head would not get larger or further brain damage occur? That was as far as I could think it through then. Yet I kept wondering about her condition – would it improve Mary's chances? Would she have any future, or would I, in some part of me, be left forever with vestiges of past grieving for what might have been?

I'd had a dream once, about my mother, who had suffered for many years from heart disease and emphysema. A certain depression hung over her. There were bad days, but mostly she would fight bravely against the depression. What I most remembered about her were her two favourite maxims: 'Be yourself, dear,' she liked to say, and 'Keep your chin up.' Mother died, quite unexpectedly, on a July morning in 1959. We found her on the floor of her room. We laid her out on her bed, stunned that she'd left us without any warning. She'd gone so suddenly that we were caught short, without any mental preparation for her death, and we all felt very guilty. I did my own share of mourning and grieving. But then one night, in the dream, I came into the dining-room and saw Mother sitting at the table. I stopped abruptly, overcome with happy surprise. 'Oh,' I said, 'you're back!' (Dreams are so matter-of-fact.) She was relaxed, her hands and elbows on the table, her eyes sparkling as though she were about to let me in on some great joke. The room was flooded with brilliant sunshine, and as I looked through the window I saw a great green stem poking out of the ground. It rose right up, its leaves unfolding, and it grew and grew until it was tall as any of the old elms and maples in the big yard. 'You know, Pat,' my mother laughed, 'things are not what they seem.' Then a pink carnation-like flower blossomed at the top, a fantastical flower that was completely and comically out of place – a huge raucous thing of incandescent green and brilliant pink. The dream vanished, but the vision remained, leaving me with two convictions – that Mother was very happy, and that things as they are hide a great Something Else that will eventually come to light in the least expected way. I never felt the need to interpret further. Nor, since then, had I ever felt any grieving kind of sorrow when thinking of my mother.

But with Mary, who was suffering so much, there was plenty to grieve about, wasn't there? She couldn't sit up. Her balance was poor. She often simply lacked energy. Her right eye still wandered off, her left arm and leg badly lagged behind her right arm and leg – and they were by no means in perfect control. In her wheelchair she still sank heavily forward or to the left. She had to be constantly reminded to sit straight and hold her head up. When she was upset she became stiff, she showed no improvement in feeding herself, and her fine-muscle co-ordination was so poor she frequently knocked over her cup.

I was so intent on her physical condition that I was unaware at first of what else was happening with Mary – in her conversation. Almost unnoticeably her stock of words began to widen. She'd spoken in baby sentences before, using a very simple shorthand kind of speech. Now she was becoming very deliberative, playing at sentences, twisting them around, using adjectives and adverbs, changing the tenses of verbs, sometimes playing, as though inspired, with her own variations. It must have been November when we first began to talk about it. And then every day one of us would have some new story about what Mary had just said.

'I think I'd ravver to have potatoes and jelly doughnuts for dinner tonight,' she'd announce in a single running breath which nearly collapsed her as she reached the end. Then she'd look up, grinning triumphantly. 'Do you mind, Muvver? Is that okay witchou?' Everyone began to notice. 'Wow!' Mark would say, looking up from his drawing of a battle scene. 'Sometimes she talks just like a big person. Not even like a kid!' Mary, fully understanding the compliment, would beam with pleasure. She began to take great delight in her appropriation of language – whole big chunks at a time now, rhythmic antithetical constructions, cadenced and inflected and often beautifully balanced.

'She's really getting sharp,' Mark would say with a solemn look.

'How about some meat Mary?' I'd interrupt, just to see what she'd say.

'No-o-o,' she'd drawl in a polite, teasing tone. 'Maybe tomorrow, if you don't mind. It's too hot for me to eat today. The meat is a bit too hot.'

'Maybe you'll change your mind,' I persisted.

'Nope.' She rocked back and forth, singing now. 'I *don't* think so. Nope. Nope. Nope.'

One morning Priscilla the cat walked into the room.

Mary, in her high-chair, looked down at her, musingly. 'Hi, Shorty,' she said.

One afternoon Mary was sitting in her orange plastic Whizwheel, a low round car mounted on three discs. She could really only manoeuvre it with her right hand but, using that hand, she was able to circle around forward, to back up, and manoeuvre her way across the kitchen floor, bumping into cabinets, backing and turning again till she'd bump into something else. While she was on the wheel that afternoon, Bonnie came in with news of some achievement at school. With a sideways look at Bonnie, Mary continued to spin. Then as Bonnie concluded her story, Mary shouted out, 'Oh, *good*, Bonnie. I'm so proud of you!' Bonnie laughed in surprise at this outcry from the blur of orange on the floor. 'Did you hear *that*?' she asked, laughing, and Mary began to shake with her own giggling.

I felt that what she said was socially as well as syntactically precocious. I thought that her saying such things, and the great care she took in saying them, showed a kind of polished courtesy we'd never expected from Mary. I was proud of her, as any parent would be, seeing a child of theirs grow to be kind and considerate and full of concern for others.

Tom and I were sitting in the living-room one night after the children had gone to bed.

'When she came from Ireland, Tom, she had a vocabulary of only ten words.'

'It must be the shunt,' he said. 'We thought it would help her physically, but instead it's helped her – *talk*!' He laughed, shaking his head. 'She's quite a little person now.'

'A character,' I said, proudly.

This was not an uninterrupted royal progress. She wasn't always *on*, by any means, but as the months went by Mary continued to be a phenomenon to us, with her wordplay and her sudden irruptions of stories, jokes and teasing. One thing Mary had become very interested in was people's names – first and last. For some strange reason, she'd had an excellent memory for names all along, and now she seemed to actively want to fix a label on each face that came to her attention.

'What's his name?' she demanded of Bonnie, who was sitting next to her on the couch, one evening. She could hardly see the screen but she recognised an anchorman on the nightly news broadcast.

'Frank – ' Bonnie began hesitantly.

'Frank? And what's his *other* name?'

Bonnie frowned, leaning forward. 'What's his last name?' she asked her father.

'Futter,' interrupted Mary, her arms waving up and down. 'Frank Futter!' and Bonnie fell back into the cushions giggling as Mary began to shake with laughter.

Putting Mary to bed one hot evening, I was struggling to keep her upright while removing her undershirt. 'Here,' I said, 'We'll take this off tonight because it's so warm. Then we'll put on something cool. All right?'

'Yes. My pink nightgown with the flowers?'

'No. That's in the wash.' I picked up one of Bonnie's old cotton nightshirts with big puffed eyelet sleeves. The material was soft and it would be loose and cool on Mary, I thought; the best thing for her on such a night. I began to put it over her head.

'I don't like it,' she said, pushing it off.

'What?' I asked. 'Why? It's very pretty.'

'No, I don't like it. It's too big – it's *stupid*.'

Despite her disapproval, she finally agreed to wear it to bed. But it *was* too big for her. She knew what she wanted, this girl. In her speech sessions at school, Mary was growing bored with certain sets of cards. Her speech therapist, Linda, had been going over material showing sequential and causal relationships – a visit to the supermarket, to the drug store, the making of an apple pie, and so on.

'Mary, you're not paying attention!' Linda finally said to her. 'What's the matter?'

'I'm sick of this,' was Mary's reply.

'What did you say?' Linda laughed, leaning back in her chair. 'You're sick of it?'

'I'm *sick* of it,' Mary said with finality.

'First we made chocolate pudding in my school today.'

'Fine, Mary,' Tom said, waiting for her to continue.

'But it didn't work, so we had chocolate *milk* to drink.'

Tom laughed at Mary's half-conscious humour, and so did I. Then Mary began to laugh too, that shaking laugh of hers, wildly pleased that she'd provoked all this merriment.

'Say it again, Mary – '

'We had chocolate pudding in school today, but it didn't work, so we drank chocolate *milk*!' Now Bonnie and Mark were laughing too, and Mary was heaving with helpless giggles.

She loved it when we laughed outright at some sally of hers. One day she was wheeling around in the kitchen. 'Excuse me,' she said. 'Is anybody hurt?'

'Oh,' I asked. 'Are you the doctor?'

'No! I'm the ambulance.'

I had to drive Mary one summer afternoon for an initial interview at the new local special education centre prior to her attending the summer school. We reached the school complex, built upon a barren place along the road leading to the expressway – no trees, only beach grass, sand pines, ice plants with purple flowers. The buildings were settled around a core of low prefab units, hastily constructed, as though a core of impermanence had been built in from the beginning and then solidified little by little. There was a flagpole with flag blowing, institutionalising the arrangement. Mary was sitting in the back seat of the car, her right arm on the armrest, propping herself up with her left hand as best she could. She had some special preference for sitting in the back seat – probably the fact that Bonnie and Mark often rode there made it seem appropriate; she was getting bigger, and therefore more like them. Her vision bounded by the looming driver's seat, she couldn't really see a great deal from back there. We'd noticed, though, that Mary had an uncanny way of knowing where she was, of locating herself in the village, even though she'd be sitting in the back seat and her head was below window level so that she couldn't see buildings. 'Oh, there's the post office!' she'd announce. Or 'We're passing Papa and Mimi's house.' She must be tracking her way by memorising treetops, was one of Tom's theories. 'How can she tell?' Mark would demand to know. He'd often be in the back seat with her, and he'd try sitting in a slumped position below the window level. He'd straighten up and look out the window to confirm what she'd said. then he would look at her in wonder. 'You're *magic*, Mary!'

That afternoon there were just the two of us going to the special education centre. I parked the car and looked back at her, huddled there. Mary, despite her handicaps, now knew how to express herself beautifully. Despite her failure to take in enough air, or to conserve it before reaching the end of a sentence, she enunciated clearly. She was capable at home of combining story with commentary, careful reports with elaborate questioning. But in public sometimes she would fall silent, and nothing any of us would say would stir her to speech. Would she talk now? The social worker, the psychologist, the occupational and speech therapists would be waiting not only to see Mary but to hear and evaluate her responses.

'We'll go in and talk to some people here, Mary,' I said. 'They want to meet you. They'll want to talk to you. And you'll talk to them.'

'I'll talk to them?' Mary repeated.

'Yes,' I said. 'They'll want to hear what you have to say.'

Getting out of the car, I went around to get Mary. I lifted out and flipped open the stroller and pressed my foot on the hinged bar between the wheels. Continuing this familiar dance routine, I released the front seat, pushed it forward and, scooping Mary up, swung her into the stroller. I closed the car door, and we were on our way.

The social worker, the woman who had signed her name to the correspondence, came to us along the hallway. Her smile was bright and there was an energy in her step. Mary wore white tights, black patent strap shoes, and a pretty dress Nannie had recently given her – light blue with tiny yellow flowers, with white smocking down the front, with big white puffed sleeves matching a gathered apron overskirt ruffled in front.

'Oh, Mary!' said the social worker. 'Such a pretty girl, and all dressed up!' Mary self-importantly smoothed her skirt.

'We'll see the psychologist and therapists first, and then I'll show you the rooms where all the boys and girls go to their classes. Is that all right with you, Mary?'

Mary's eyes were alight. She was so excited that her 'yes' was lost in an explosion of air. Again I worried about her being able to talk during the interview. We were taken to a carpeted office, with desk and a big table and chairs, where the psychologist and two therapists were waiting. The therapists were pretty young women, the phsychologist a stout round-faced man with black glasses framing his dark eyes. The purpose of the brief meeting was to let these people see and hear Mary, and ask me questions about her. After they'd made their assessment, we were to see the physical set-up. Mary would then see the doctor, who would have me sign a sheet releasing Mary's records from St Charles so that Mary could attend the summer programme here.

I settled Mary, still in her stroller, in front of the table next to the social worker. 'This is Mary Collins,' she began, and the others smiled and nodded. It was hard for them to know how to react. They had never seen Mary, and wouldn't know much about her condition – whether she was retarded, or emotionally disturbed, or perhaps given to fits of crying. They were cautious, guarded, expectant.

'How old are you, Mary,' the psychologist asked.

'I'm five,' Mary said in a loud voice, sitting forward now in her seat. 'At my last birthday I was five.'

I felt relieved. 'That's fine, Mary,' I said, moving in the chair. You can tell them – '

'You don't talk, Mom!' Mary loudly interrupted. Frowning sternly at me, Mary dropped her right hand emphatically on to her knee. 'I'm going to talk.' She raised her hand and slapped her knee again. 'Now,' she said, looking directly at the psychologist. 'What is your name?'

'My name?' He laughed, then gave his name.

She studied him for a moment. Then she turned and lifted her finger and pointed to the first therapist. 'And what is *your* name?' she demanded. The young woman answered her. Imperiously, Mary turned to the other therapist, sitting between the social worker and psychologist. 'And yours?' The young woman gave her name. 'How old are you?' Mary asked. 'I'm twenty-eight,' she answered.

'Oh,' Mary seemed satisfied. She sat back, having decided, apparently, that it was time for them to question her. 'You can talk now,' she announced.

'Where do you live, Mary?' asked the psychologist.

'I live in Westhampton Beach. In a house.'

I couldn't say anything, and didn't want to, as I was delighted to watch this scene unfold, with Mary playing the leading role.

'Do you have any brothers and sisters?'

'My sister Bonnie, and my brother Mark.'

'Would you like to go to school here?'

'To summer school? Yes. I would like that.'

'We would like to have you. Do you know that?'

'Yes,' Mary said, with a laugh and a snort. 'I know that. Are we finished now?'

'Do you want to see the classrooms where the girls and boys learn?'

'Yes!' she answered, nearly bouncing out of her stroller.

You Light Up My Life

At home one evening Mary was playing with a yellow potholder, woven by Bonnie on a small loom she'd received for Christmas.

'This is the exercise mat,' she said, turning it over and over and patting it. 'Oh!' She became very excited. 'Oh, Paf! *I forgot.* I need my dolly!' ('I forgot' meant that something important had just occurred to her, and 'Paf' meant 'Pat' – calling me by my first name in imitation of her father.)

'Your dolly's upstairs,' I said. I was taking out pots and pans from a lower shelf.

'Now,' she said urgently.

'I have to fix dinner, Mary.'

'Can you get it for me, Paf? I have the mat. The dolly *has* to do her exercises – '

I didn't have the heart to postpone her plans, so I went upstairs and dug the small doll out of the bottom of a hamper full of toys. The principal features of this doll, which was no more than six inches high, were long eyelashes, long brown stringy hair, and prominent breasts. It was made of bendable plastic, so that its legs could be bent in various ways. Mary had discovered that by jamming it forward at an angle she could make the doll sit down, and that by using both hands she could straighten it again. The doll's arms were easy to flip up and down; its head could be turned all the way around; the top half of its torso could be moved in one direction while the bottom half was being moved in another. Mary had inherited it from Bonnie, who'd spent many childhood hours with the

230

doll, dressing it and combing its hair, twisting it about just so, and then swinging the lever of a little battery-operated platform that made the doll swing as Bonnie sang her version of some pop tune. 'She's a teenager,' Bonnie would say – though the doll, with her painted face looked more like a lady of the evening.

The platform was gone now, and Mary used the doll to recreate her 'work' in school. She spoke childlike encouragements, mimicking the therapists. 'Good girl, up now, hold your head *up*. That's it! Fine – you're okay.' When the doll slipped from her hand and fell, Mary seized it and straightened its legs again. 'I'm walking, I'm walking,' she said in a tiny voice. 'Do you see me walking?' And then, in a bigger voice, 'Goo-ood! Good for you.' 'Now I'm jumping!' she said, her voice tiny again, and bounced the doll, hair flipping up and down, on and off the potholder exercise mat. Mary paid no attention to me. She was wholly caught up in her fantasy.

'Will you say "yay" for me?' she used to ask, her face alight. 'If I eat all my dinner, and drink all my milk, will you say "yay"?'

'Yes, Mary,' one of us would say.

Then she'd attack her dish industriously, scooping up her meat, usually mixed with mashed potatoes to make it easier for her to handle. Her style was to grip her spoon and, twisting her wrist, push the food ahead like a snowplough till she had a pile of it ready; then she'd circle around, bringing the spoon to her mouth; she'd empty it, and begin the ploughing again. Considering all the difficulties, she usually did quite well. When she wanted to, she could eat everything, even to chasing down the last elusive little mound of potato on her dish. Then she'd bounce up, stiffened legs swinging out. 'I'm finished!' she'd announce in a loud voice. It was our cue.

'Yay-ay-ay-ay-ay for Ma-a-a-ry!' we'd cry out in unison, and she'd fall back against her backrest, helplessly pleased, her body jiggling as she laughed and laughed.

One day she said that she didn't want Pampers any more.

'You don't need them?'

'Nope.'

'Are you sure?'

'Yep.'

And she didn't use them again, except for safety on long trips, and except for night time.

'And that's only because you can't get to the bathroom by yourself, isn't that it?'

'Yep.' Then she frowned and added, 'But I'm big?'

'Yes, you are. You're getting very big.'

Soon I noticed that half the time she'd be completely dry in the morning.

Mary had a small white plastic seat which fitted on top of the toilet and had a vinyl strap with a buckle which would hold her on securely. The door to the bathroom open, she'd sit there after dinner, her feet swinging, talking or singing to herself, until suddenly she'd shout, 'I did it! I did it!' Bonnie and Mark would run to her. 'Yay-ay-ay-ay for Mary!' they'd cry out in response. Mark would flick the bathroom light off and on, Bonnie loudly sounding the notes of the Washington Post March ('*da*-da-*da* da-da-*da*-da-da-*da*'), as they both stamped their feet. ('What do you want, a brass band?' I used to say to the older children when they were small. And here for Mary they'd devised their own version of one.) With all that applause, it was no wonder she performed this nightly ritual so successfully.

There was an accident one evening, though. I was away and after supper Tom asked Bonnie to watch over Mary while she was sitting on the toilet. Tom had not thought to strap her into her special plastic seat. Bonnie became distracted and left the bathroom for a minute or so. Mary was sitting there singing. But half a minute later she toppled forward and, unable to protect herself, landed face first on the floor. Tom had rushed in, followed by Bonnie. Tom picked her up. She had a terrible nose-bleed. Seeing the blood Bonnie was seized with remorse. She became panicky and then hysterical, running through the house screaming and shrieking. Tom staunched the nose-bleed. Sitting on the tub edge he held Mary, rocking her back and forth. Mary, who had been screaming at first, began to subside as she heard Bonnie's screaming. Tom called Bonnie in. 'She'll be all right,' he said. Lifting her bloody face, Mary said, 'Oh, Bonnie, don't cry. Please don't cry, Bonnie. It was an accident. I'll be all right.' Bonnie came to Mary, and Mary began patting her hand, anxious to calm her older sister. 'It's okay, Bonnie. Bonnie?' Bonnie stopped screaming, her fear that Mary was injured dislodged by this effort of her little sister's to comfort her.

'I felt so sorry for Mary,' Bonnie said to me later.

'And Mary felt so sorry for you,' I said.

'Yes,' she said, with a rueful little half-laugh. 'I couldn't cry any more when Mary started to pat my hand!'

Mark, four and a half years older than Mary, was more nearly a peer when he played with her. He'd take the sofa pillows and pile them up around her, making a little house. She'd sit in there without a sound, waiting for her next cue. 'It's raining!' Mark would say. 'Got to go in now. The storm is coming!' and he'd dive in next to her and they'd sit together covered completely, pillows piled above and around them. Sooner or later he'd put his head out. 'Come back in, Mark,' she'd squeal. 'Hurry up. It's *raining*!'

Mark often told her stories in which she was the main

character. But they were invariably his stories: '. . . And then Mary rode up in her tank, aiming her gun, and she shot them all dead.' Mary would breathe hard, listening intently to what he was describing, nodding her head, accepting all the warlike behaviour attributed to her. 'Yes, yes,' she'd say hoarsely, as the story mounted to its crescendo of blood and ruin.

Mark would let her use his favourite toys, offering them one by one, cautioning her as to their proper care. Whenever she was concentrating, she'd have a saliva problem. 'Don't dribble on them, now – ' he'd say.

'I won't,' she'd quickly promise.

'Swallow!' he'd command her, and she'd gulp several times. Satisfied with her sincere obedience, he'd hand over the toy.

There were plenty of interesting exchanges between the two of them. One day Mark was telling her a story. She kept breaking in to ask this and that, and he kept telling her to stop interrupting. Finally the story was finished.

Mary: 'Okay, Mark. Can I turn my mouth on now?'

Mark (exasperated): 'Yes! You can talk now. So keep quiet!'

Another time at the dinner table, Mary had been talking with her mouth full of food.

Mark: Mary, don't be a pig!

Mary (swallowing): I'm *not*.

Mark (persisting, teasing): Yes, you are.

Mary (triumphantly): No, no. I'm a pig*let*!

'Would you like a drink of milk, sweetheart Mark?'

'Oh, yes, sweetheart Mary,' he'd say brightly, mimicking her.

'No!' Mary would say. 'You don't call me sweetheart. I call *you* sweetheart!'

'Okay, Mary. Okay.'

About some things she was determined to be independent. Mary liked to sit on the edges of chairs – anywhere. Because her balance was poor this was always precarious. 'Look at me,' she'd say proudly, sitting forward very straight, her legs dangling over the edge, her head held high. 'I'm sitting up!' One of us, seeing her sway towards danger, would reach out a steadying hand. 'No, no,' she'd snap indignantly. 'Don't touch me. Please get your hand off my shoulder.'

In the car she'd usually sit next to Bonnie. As we drove along, she'd begin inching and pulling herself forward. Bonnie would move to protect her.

'Mommy, Mommy! Bonnie's touching me! Tell her to stop!'

'But Mary, she wants to help you.'

'No, no!'

'Please, Mary, you might fall.'

'I'm sitting all by *myself*!' she'd say.

She was in the kitchen in her wheelchair all alone one day. She'd been very quiet. Wondering why, I went to her. There was that expression on her face – a broader smile, her cheeks plumped up, her eyes shining – that let me know she'd done something she was particularly proud of.

She didn't say anything – she couldn't because her wide, wide grin left her speechless with pride and pleasure. Then when I looked at her feet – her red-stockinged feet – I saw what it was. She'd removed both her sneakers; she'd also removed the laces from the eyelets – so thoroughly had she done the job. The shoes and laces lay in a tumble on the footrest.

'Your shoes, Mary! You took off your shoes all by yourself!'

'Yes!' she squeaked, her head bobbing up and down.

Her ambition often took the form of trying to assist me, in the kitchen, which was the only room in the house where Mary could wheel around with some freedom. There was that broad area enclosed by the refrigerator, oven, stove, counters and the telephone wall. She learned how to release the brakes on the wheelchair. First, leaning over to her right, she threw off the rubber-handled brake there. Then she leaned to the left, struggling with her left hand to release the brake on that side. Still too small to reach the two brakes simultaneously, neither could she reach the two wheels at once. She had to wheel first in a half circle with her right hand and then in a half circle with her left until finally, laboriously, she'd put the chair where she wanted it. She'd go to the kitchen utensil drawers on a level with her head and, busily opening them, announce that she was going to help. She'd remove the stainless steel cutlery from one drawer with her right hand, carefully placing knives, forks and spoons on the countertop. She'd then go to another drawer, the kitchen drawer that had become a kind of catch-all – originally a drawer for large utensils like ladles, openers, stirrers, spatulas but also containing corks, scissors, matches and all sorts of other odds and ends. Going through this drawer gave her special delight.

'Oh, I found you some stwing, Paf,' she'd say. 'I'll put it up on the counter so you can use it, okay?' Her manner would be conspiratorial, helpful, cajoling – and patronising.

Tiring of that after a while, she'd wheel over to the cabinets 'to go to the store'.

'I need a shopping bag, Paf.' I'd give her a brown bag from our assortment of grocery bags tucked away in a lower cabinet, and she'd try to angle herself to open the lower cabinet without the wheelchair getting in the way.

Sometimes she just couldn't do it. 'I'm stuck,' she'd whisper apologetically. Or 'The door *can't* open.' Very difficult for her – an admission of failure. So I'd drop what I was doing and go over and wheel her into a parking arrangement in front of the cabinet, with the doors wide open and the right side of the chair close to the shelves. 'Thank you,' she'd say formally. 'Now, I'll just do a little shopping for you. Do you want peas, Paf?'

Mary had a friend, Kevin – a boy whom she described as doing outrageous and naughty things – spilling his milk, pouring water on the floor, screaming at the teacher, refusing to eat his lunch. He often teased and tormented and even tortured her. At first we thought Kevin was real – an unruly older child, perhaps, in her class at the clinic school. But he kept appearing under different guises. Sometimes he was a girl. Sometimes he was her fingers, standing up on the lapboard and walking from one side to the other, or fingers walking up my chest, neck and face as I held her. 'Stop that, Mary! It tickles!'

'It's Kevin.'

'Tell him to stop.'

'He doesn't want to stop.'

'Then he's naughty.'

Mary would nod her head up and down, her eyes gleaming with her concurrence in my low opinion of this wild child of her imagination. Most often he'd do wrong, break laws, defy authority, and get away with it. But sometimes she saw to it that he was given the harsh treatment he deserved for his well-advertised depradations. She had his bad reputation to inspire her whenever it suited her to use him as a whipping boy, and she took malicious pleasure seeing to it he was properly punished. Every privilege or advantage Mary enjoyed was heightened by the fact that it was denied Kevin.

'We're going out for pizza tonight,' Mark would announce to her delight.

'But Kevin's *not*!' Mary would immediately say.

'You can stay up till eight tonight,' I'd announce.

'I can but Kevin *can't*,' she'd promptly say. 'Kevin has to go to bed.'

'You children have a treat tonight after dinner,' I'd say, planning ice-cream sandwiches.

'Kevin's sick,' she'd say. 'He can't have any.'

Yet he was hers, and she seemed to have a soft spot for him. Or perhaps it was that she merely wanted to press her advantage, squeeze out the satisfaction of her superior good fortune. Sometimes, when we'd leave the house for some adventure, she could be heard gently murmuring, 'Bye, Kevin.'

Mary liked to publicly rejoice in her moral superiority to real children who misbehaved.

'David was bad today.'

'Oh? What did he do?'

'He didn't listen.'

'He didn't?'

'And the other kids – they don't pay attention.'

'But of course *you* do,' I teased.

'Yes!' She bounced vigorously in her chair.

'Good.'

'But I'm the only one,' she said.

These stratagems were, as much as anything, an effort to establish her own worth. Mary would often say, 'I'm a *person*.' And she seemed to have a very precise idea of what that meant.

Afternoons when she was resting, and when she lay in her crib late on Saturday mornings, she'd have Kevin and countless others as guests. Sometimes there'd be conversation, sometimes heated argument. Often singing and carolling. From the sound of things, phantoms of all of us would be guests at these feasts, and phantoms of other people Mary had met lately or long ago. During the summer, when she was more rested, or after a series of holidays, she took to holding late night gatherings. We'd wake up, hearing a shriek, but it would be of pleasure rather than of pain – a party of Mary's going full blast. Then one of us would go in to Mary and remind her that others were sleeping. She'd smile the sweetest smile, pleased no doubt, that her extravagant celebrating had made her so notorious as to bring this plea for calm. Invariably she'd quieten down. Eventually she'd sleep. But often she'd proceed – except with instructions now to the guests at her nocturnal revels to do their whooping in lowered voices and carry on their carousals in more subdued tones. I used to wonder whether she had any idea how delighted we were about these parties of hers – evidence of so much imagination, testimony to a glad and joyous spirit.

Mary's delight and enthusiasm were contagious. One day Bonnie carted her off to the local pizzeria, Bonnie piloting the 'Bugger' attached to her bicycle. This facility, however unfortunate its name, was a small, beautifully balanced steel contraption with traces that could be attached to a bicycle much in the fashion that the traces of a trap are hooked up to a horse. With its black plastic seat and two wheels, it functioned as an upright baby carriage, a kind of landau. When Mary rode off she'd be sitting up, leaning deliberately against the blue pillow, her arms outstretched so that she could balance herself upright on the plastic armrests.

When Bonnie returned that day she was breathlessly excited. So eager was she to tell us what happened that she'd left Mary sitting in her horseless carriage out in the driveway. Bonnie and I went out to Mary. She looked pleased and happy, rocking gently back and forth, staring up at the sky. I turned my attention to Bonnie, who, jumping up and down, was full of her story.

'You know how much Mary likes "You Light Up My Life"?'

'Oh, yes.' It was Mary's favourite then. She knew all the lyrics and would lift her voice and belt them out, not very tunefully, whenever the mood was on her.

'Well, we sat down near the jukebox. I got the high chair for Mary, and set up everything, and ordered our pizza. Then I played three songs, you know, and the last was "You Light Up My Life". I picked that one for Mary. Well, the pizza came and we were just sitting there eating, the two of us, and all of a sudden Mary heard her song playing! She was so surprised she stopped eating. She started to sing out – and her voice was really loud. Then the people at the next table joined in, to help her along. Then the waitresses. And Mommy, and then – ' Bonnie's voice rose higher, 'all the other people in the room started singing it, too! The whole place singing "You Light Up My Life". For Mary!'

It was Mary's fearlessness and determination again. Partly because she was so handicapped, I suppose, her elation and buoyancy seemed to have a powerful effect on other people. And yet she wasn't that self-conscious about her winsomeness – at least she wasn't yet. She accepted their interest, their curiosity, their helpfulness with perfect nonchalance. She was, I used to think, like a beautiful woman accepting compliments – graciously, and yet as no more than her due.

A Hovering Presence

'I'll see you later, Daddy,' Mary said one day, in a warm voice and all in one breath, as Tom went upstairs to resume his work. I was standing in the kitchen. It was three in the afternoon and Mary, just in from summer school, sat parked in her wheelchair under the wall telephone. She was slumped forward on to the lapboard, resting on her elbows, eating her snack. Seized in her too-tight grip, pinched by the fingers of her right hand, was a bread and butter square. She took a bite, glancing up towards the window. 'Hold your head up, Mary,' I said. She tried to, and then slumped back again, lost in some reflection or daydream.

It was very still in the kitchen. As I was standing watching her, I began to see a kind of pattern emerge, conditioned by what was there in the room, an impression woven of touch and smell and taste and sound but a single pattern, the kind that creates a tapestry. It was a seeing that went beyond the sense impressions themselves. Here we were, Mary and I, in this funny carriage house kitchen with its jutting counter with its tile roof laid over horses' boards, with its varying sized window frames above what had been horse stalls ninety years ago. Here we were in this silly big kitchen with its soft wainscotting of pine, with the refrigerator standing primly and the rogue unreliable oven tucked in next to it, and the old stovetop with the ever present kettle, paint peeling from it; with the towel rack above, potholder mitts and rubber gloves draping from it like paws; with salt, pepper, sauces, nutmeg, ginger and cloves sitting on a tin tray on the outsize countertop; with the dishes in the sink; with the dryer over there – jeans, shirts, socks and towels clattering and thumping in it; with the drawing table and fluorescent lamp both dusty with lint from the dryer; and with that disused old relic of a metal kitchen table with its red and white chequerboard plastic cloth laden with books, games, folded clothes and the sewing box.

What I suddenly seemed to see amid all this kitchen panorama was a bending-over and hovering presence, encircling and enfolding little Mary in some intensity of desire. Mary, I saw, was caught in this presence, she lived and moved in it, the focus of its burning and passionate longing. It was whispering to her in a flow of pride and delight, as a parent bends over a first-born, foolishly crooning and babbling noises of encouragement and praise, cradling the small head and idiotically scrutinising the tiny face for some fleeting sign of recognition. I thought I saw then how this being bends over all creatures, itself becomes all suffering, and by sheer explosive intensity of desire and will brings the creature into the full light, so that all they could be and ever longed and yearned to be, even the tiniest slightest desire, is realised. And I saw, as Dame Julian of Norwich seemed to say, that this playing out of each creature's possibilities would be endless and that the result would be sheer delight.

The windows were open and outdoors there was the mid-August buzz and din and chirping of crickets. Mary looked down as the cat came mincing in, forepaws daintily crisscrossing, whiskers twitching as she paused to rub the rim of Mary's wheelchair parked next to the doorway beside the phone. The cat strolled beyond the counter, disappearing behind it in search of some tidbit, unaware of what was happening in the room, unaware of the silent music – loud, wild music as from a calliope, although there was no sound. There were the colours, too: an infinity of rainbow colours, no spectrum displayed but glowing and spreading like a haze of fire. As Mary sat there, rolling her unfocused eyes, I knew that she was not a machine some of whose parts didn't work, not a discard from the assembly plant. Everywhere I felt fullness, satisfaction, pleasure, comfort, and I faintly understood why the Israelites chose the images of pillar of fire and cloud and above all whirlwind. There was energy here like the whirlwind, but attentive, concerned, fascinated, enraptured. Mary was the delight and pleasure of some infinite being, who regarded her as though she were the centre of the universe, as though the sun and moon and all planets and stars in all distant galaxies had all been created for her as had the breeze that carried in the sounds of leaves and insects and birdsong, as had the solemn cat returning, its eyes suddenly iridescent as they caught the sunlight, to rub against the counter stool and to look up again at Mary.

'Please, Mary, hold your head up,' I said. As I spoke, I shattered the silence, and the woven strands of the fabric made of fleeting impressions dissolved, coalescing briefly and then vanishing in the sunlight. But now, finally, I'd had a chance to understand. Mary couldn't hold her head up. It was a symbol of her damage, of all her muscular disabilities, this inability to hold her head up. Her head was all the way down now instead of up, she was slumped completely forward, her left cheek lay resting on her left fist as her right hand moved another square of bread to her mouth. But she was perking up now. 'Do you want some, Honey Mommy?' she asked me, holding out the piece of bread. I was smiling at her solicitous tone. 'Honey Mary, Please,' I said. 'Please hold your head up!' I think it was out of sympathy for me that she did lift her head, and then fully straighten herself up, leaning against the backrest so that her chin was tucked in below her face. She was all the way up now. She looked at me impishly over the rims of her glasses.

'No!' she said, wildly waving the soggy wad of bread for emphasis. 'You don't call *me* honey. I call *you* honey!'

In a place beyond the limits of our time, Mary's arms would reach out more easily and her fingers and hands would seize and hold the universe itself. She would do intricate work. She would speak clearly and perfectly. She would see all that could possibly be seen and know all things. She would sing out with a full-throated voice. She would walk; she would run and go and fling herself across the galaxies for sheer delight.

And she would hold her head up, high.

[This] little thing, the size of a hazelnut . . . I wondered how long it could last; for it seemed as though it might suddenly fade away to nothing, it was so small. And I was answered in my understanding: 'It lasts, and ever shall last; for God loveth it. And even so hath everything being – by the love of God.'

Julian of Norwich

LIFE HAD PASSED HER BY. UNTIL
SHE DARED TO TAKE HER LIFE
INTO HER OWN HANDS...

REVELATIONS
PHYLLIS NAYLOR

Mary is unmarried, the secretary of the Faith
Holiness congregation, and for thirty-four years
has led a model life. She has nursed her
crippled mother, stood by her family when her
wild, beloved brother defied the church and fled
to California. And she is resigned to the
prospect that life has passed her by . . . forever.

Until the sudden arrival of her free-thinking,
young nephew throws her world into turmoil.
Bright, affectionate and vulnerable, thirteen-
year-old Jake joins forces with Mary's out-
spoken girlfriend in opposing the gospel
according to Faith Holiness. And sets Mary on
the path of deliciously sinful liberation that
reveals a funny, feminine personality whose
search for fulfilment is strewn with . . .

REVELATIONS

GENERAL FICTION   0 7221 6323 1   £1.50

A Nurse's War

BY BRENDA McBRYDE
(illustrated)

IT TOOK COURAGE TO LIVE THROUGH IT –
AND COURAGE TO WRITE ABOUT IT

Brenda McBryde's uniquely moving story began on the eve of
World War II when she enrolled as a trainee nurse at the
Royal Victoria Infirmary, Newcastle. The next six years saw
Sister McBryde nursing civilians through the Blitz,
volunteering for service in the Maxillo-Facial ('Max-Factor')
plastic surgery unit, joining the troops in the early days
following the D-Day landings, and serving in the Field
Hospitals in the front line of fighting. Then, as the war drew
to a close, she faced the greatest challenge of her career:
the restoration to health and sanity of Germany's
concentration camp victims.

'This book clutches the heart'
Cambridge Evening News

AUTOBIOGRAPHY   0 7221 5774 6   £1.25

A SELECTION OF BESTSELLERS FROM SPHERE

FICTION

CALIFORNIA DREAMERS	Norman Bogner	£1.75 ☐
HEART OF WAR	John Masters	£1.95 ☐
TUNNEL WAR	Joe Poyer	£1.50 ☐
LOVING	Danielle Steel	£1.50 ☐
REVELATIONS	Phyllis Naylor	£1.50 ☐

FILM & TV TIE-INS

THE FUNHOUSE	Owen West	£1.25 ☐
THE EMPIRE STRIKES BACK	Donald F. Glut	£1.00 ☐
BUCK ROGERS IN THE 25TH CENTURY	Addison E. Steele	95p ☐
LLOYD GEORGE	David Benedictus	£1.25 ☐

NON-FICTION

MARY	Patricia Collins	£1.50 ☐
EAGLE DAY	Richard Collier	£4.75 ☐
THE CLASSIFIED MAN	Susanna M. Hoffman	£1.50 ☐
WILL	G. Gordon Liddy	£1.75 ☐
MY LIFE AND GAME	Bjorn Borg	£1.25 ☐